# THE FIRST COMPLETE
# MARKETING GUIDE FOR CAMPGROUNDS

# THE FIRST COMPLETE MARKETING GUIDE FOR CAMPGROUNDS

William Fillman

Sagamore Publishing Co. Inc.
Champaign, Illinois 61824–0673

Book Design: Judith Saak
Cover Design: Michelle Dressen
Photographs: Brian Moore
Editors: Joyce Meyer and Karen Walker
Back Cover Copy: Lisa Kingery

Printed in the United States of America


Library of Congress Catalog Card Number: 90-62006
ISBN: 0-915611-33-3

# TABLE OF CONTENTS

# LIST OF FORMS

# INTRODUCTION

What can marketing do for your campground business? Since selling began, both small and large business owners have been awed, confused and frustrated by the concept of "marketing" their products. The term itself is often associated with textbook theories, mathematical formulas and technical analysis of the workings of the economy as a whole. You may even think it's something that's a concern only for large national companies.

In its simplest and most practical form, though, marketing is involved in what you do every day as a business owner or manager. Whether you're running a giant corporation or a family-owned campground, the profitability of your business depends on how successful you are at attracting paying customers. And that's really the essence of marketing. Marketing is everything you do to promote and sell your product or service to people who will pay you for it.

# BASICS FOR BUSINESS

The idea behind marketing starts with a simple analysis of what you have and what you need. To understand the role of marketing in your business, think first of what you have to sell. Like all businesses, your campground has only four possible things to sell to potential customers:

Product — the campground's physical features and benefits.

Service — the additional courtesies, considerations and privileges you provide to your customers.

Location — where it is.

Price — what it costs your customers to use it.

Even though you can offer all four of these elements, it's unlikely that all of them are truly worth "selling." Developing and carrying out a marketing plan will help you evaluate your campground's features through your customer's eyes. You'll learn what your real advantages are and how you should be promoting them.

Now consider what you need to keep your business operating. There are three major requirements:

Product — something needed or wanted by potential customers.

Financing — money to develop and maintain your campground and cover ongoing business expenses.

Marketing — a way to let potential customers know your product exists and show them how it meets their needs or desires.

Most business owners are very familiar with their product's physical features and the money they need to run their business, and they know they have to promote their product. The real mystery is the way to promote it — a system for collecting good information about what you have and deciding which marketing activities will be most successful in selling it.

A good marketing system always involves the use of a written plan, which is the focus of this guide. A good plan will organize your day-to-day selling activities and show you how you can spend less money to achieve better results. It gives you a way of checking your progress and correcting problems. And it shows you how to take advantage of new opportunities that can make your campground business even more profitable.

## A Marketing Plan Just for Campground Owners and Managers

Whether you've been in operation for years or are considering opening a new campground, this guide gives you all the "how to's" involved in developing your own marketing plan. This is not a general marketing manual — it's a step-by-step plan that will help you handle the special marketing problems you face as a campground owner or manager.

You'll see the practical benefits as you progress through the chapters in this guide. It will take you through all the steps involved in collecting information and developing your marketing plan. You'll learn how to come up with a realistic budget and how to plan the advertising and promotional activities you've decided on. Also featured here are tips for preparing your ads and a system for handling inquiries from potential customers.

The guide provides a built-in method of organizing your plan and recording your progress. Because nothing exists until it is written down, the guide includes easy-to-use forms to help you keep track of the information you develop at each step. At the end of the book, you'll find out how to evaluate what you've done and make plans for the next season.

# 1    GETTING STARTED: DEVELOPING THE MARKETING PLAN

Marketing plans can vary greatly in complexity and scope, but all businesses — from multi-national corporations to small "mom and pop" enterprises — begin essentially with the same three steps. This simple but effective approach makes use of many sources of information that are already available, so it doesn't require any great expenditure from you.

In its simplest form, your marketing plan will make use of your answers to these three questions:

1. Who is your customer? (Step 1: Define the Customer)

2. What are you up against? (Step 2: Analyze the Competition)

3. What do you have to offer? (Step 3: Evaluate the Product)

# STEP 1: DEFINING THE CUSTOMER

The first — and most important — step in any marketing plan is determining who your customers are. It's not feasible or cost-effective to talk to everyone, so you need to narrow the field to the specific types of customers who are most likely to use your campground. Your goal is to spend your marketing dollars reaching only those customers who offer the greatest potential for sales and profits.

## Using the Customer Definition Form

One of the best ways to categorize campground customers is by the types of campers they use. The form on the opposite page will help you organize your information. The major types of campers are listed in the left-hand column, with space for other categories that may apply in your special situation.

For each camper type, fill in the approximate number of customers who use your campground each year. You can get these numbers from previous years' records or, if this information isn't available, make an educated guess. The important thing is to determine the relative numbers of each type.

Now look at your estimates and determine who your "best" customers are. Most of your customers may fall into just one or two categories, or you may see several types that are responsible for most of your business. For the purposes of your marketing plan, you want to target the customer type that offers the greatest potential for future use of your campground.

You may choose to target just one group or several, but in most cases, each customer category will require a different type of marketing effort. For example, your completed form may show you that recreational vehicles and tent campers accounted for most of your business last year. It's unlikely that you'll be able to use the same advertising and promotions to attract both types of customers. Recreational vehicle owners are interested in different campground features and advantages than tent campers are. They read different publications and may respond to your promotions in very different ways.

Now that you know who your best potential customers are, it's important to find out as much as you can about them — what they're looking for in a campground, how often they camp, what publications they read regularly. You need to collect this information for each group you've chosen to target. You can use a number of published sources to gather this marketing information. Here are some good places to start.

| CUSTOMER/MARKET DEFINITION FORM | | | | | |
|---|---|---|---|---|---|
| | | POTENTIAL CUSTOMERS | WEEK-DAY | WEEK-END | PERCENTAGE FOR YEAR | DISTANCE THEY TRAVELED TO GET TO YOUR FACILITY |
| 1. | TENTS | | | | | |
| 2. | POP UP/ PULL UP CAMPERS | | | | | |
| 3. | TRAILERS | | | | | |
| 4. | PICKUP TRUCK MTD | | | | | |
| 5. | TRAILERS | | | | | |
| 6. | 5TH WHEEL | | | | | |
| 7. | RVS | | | | | |
| 8. | MOTORCYCLES | | | | | |
| 9. | GROUPS | | | | | |
| 10. | OTHER | | | | | |
| 11. | OTHER | | | | | |
| 12. | OTHER | | | | | |

## Camping Magazines

The easiest and most obvious sources are the magazines that your customer reads. Every group of customers that you have defined has a special publication designed for its special camping interest.

Take recreational vehicle owners, for instance. How do you find out which magazines they are reading? The easiest way to determine which ones are most popular is to ask your customers — talk to the family who's parked in your campground and ask them what RV magazines they read.

Now what do you want to know about RV people? Every question you might have has probably been answered by the research departments of the magazines that RV enthusiasts are reading. These magazines have gone to great lengths to define their customers, and what they know about their readers is likely to correspond to what you want to know about your potential campground customers. Magazines use this data, which is updated often, to sell their advertising space and to ensure that their feature articles are of interest to their readers.

To get this information, use your campground letterhead to write to the magazine's advertising department. Ask for a "media kit," which is a package of information for advertisers. A sample letter for this purpose is included on the opposite page.

In addition to the magazine's advertising rates, these kits usually include an editorial calendar, a sample issue and detailed information about its readers. Media Kits from two camping magazines are shown here.

# YOUR LETTERHEAD

Date

*Motor Home*
Tl Enterprises, Inc., Publication
29901 Agoura Rd.
Agoura, CA 91301

Dear Client Services Representative:

I am requesting a copy of the media kit for *Motor Home* and a recent issue of the publication. Thank you.

Sincerely,

Name and
Title

*Using the Media Analysis Form*

As you collect information about the various magazines, record it on the Media Analysis form included here. The form provides you with an easy-to-read summary of which magazines your customers are reading. Write down the magazines' total circulations and a breakdown of their circulations to your defined customers. If your targeted customers are RV owners, for example, record this number on the line provided on the form. The number of RV owners who read the magazine is going to be more important to you than the total number of readers.

While you're recording reader information, jot down the advertising rates, deadlines and "CPM" — the cost of reaching 1000 readers with an ad in the magazine. (To figure CPM, multiply the cost of an ad by 1000 and divide by the number of your defined customers — not necessarily the total circulation — the magazine reaches). This information will be valuable later when you're making decisions about placing ads.

## MEDIA ANALYSIS FORM

PUBLICATION    _____    _____    _____

EDITORIAL PROFILE    _____    _____    _____

_____    _____    _____

_____    _____    _____

_____    _____    _____

EDITORS    _____    _____    _____

_____    _____    _____

REP YOUR AREA    _____    _____    _____

COST B&W PAGE    _____    _____    _____

CPM*    _____    _____    _____

FORMAT: PAGE SIZE    _____    _____    _____

PUBLICATION FREQUENCY    _____    _____    _____

DEADLINE    _____    _____    _____

CIRCULATION    _____    _____    _____

CONTROLLED    _____    _____    _____

PAID    _____    _____    _____

• • • • • • • • • • • • • • • • • • • • • • • • • • • • • • • • • • • • • • • •

PRIMARY CIRCULATION    _____    _____    _____

_____    _____    _____

_____    _____    _____

_____    _____    _____

_____    _____    _____

_____    _____    _____

TOTAL    _____    _____    _____

*CPM FORMULA: $\dfrac{\text{COST} \times 1{,}000}{\text{CIRCULATION}} = $ COST PER THOUSAND (CPM )

*Your Local Library*

If you want to learn even more about the different publications your potential customers are reading, you can find detailed information in your local library. Usually located in the reference section, the Standard Rate & Data Service (SRDS) volumes classify publications by reader interest. Find the volume for Consumer Magazines and use Section 8A, "Campers, RV, Motor Home & Trailers." Jot down the names of all the magazines that you think might be read by your customers.

Sample SRDS pages for recreational vehicle publications are shown on pages 9–10. You can get a good idea of the magazine's content from the publisher's description under the Editorial Profile heading. The listings also give you circulation breakdowns of the types and numbers of campers who are reading each publication. Choose the magazines that you think are most popular among your targeted customers, and record information about them on the Media Analysis form. Make copies of the form if you've chosen more than three magazines.

## 8 Business & Finance
## 8A Campers, Recreational Vehicles, Motor Homes & Trailers

### WORLD MONITOR

Mid 045867-000

1 Norway St., Boston, MA 02115. Phone 617-450-2000. FAX: 617-450-2654, .
See listing under classification No. 22.

## 8A Campers, Recreational Vehicles, Motor Homes & Trailers

**See also: 8B-Camping & Outdoor Recreation; 19-Fishing & Hunting; 45-Sports; 46-Travel**

### Adventure Road

The

200 E. Randolph I
2583. FAX: 312
See listing under c

**PUBLICATION**

00
6-

### CHEVY OUTDOORS

BPA Consumer Audit

Mid 041862-0

3221 West Big Beaver, Suite 110, Troy, MI 48084. Ph
313-643-7050.
See lis

Fa

**EDITORIAL PROFILE**

Media ... )

Published monthly by Family Motor Coach Assoc., 8291 Clough Pike, Cincinnati, OH 45244. Phone 513-474-3622.

**PUBLISHER'S EDITORIAL PROFILE**

FAMILY MOTOR COACHING Magazine is edited for the members and prospective members of the Family Motor Coach Association who own or about to purchase recreational vehicles of the motor coach style and use them exclusively for pleasure. Featured are articles on travel and recreations, association news; meetings, activities, and conventions plus articles on new products. Approximately 1/3 of editorial content is devoted to travel and entertainment, 1/3 to Association news, and 1/3 to new products and industry news.

**1. PERSONNEL**
Editor—Pamela Wisby-Kay.
Publisher/Mgr.—Virginia Bauman.

**2. REPRESENTATIVES and/or BRANCH OFFICES**
Denver, Dallas, Portland, San Francisco, Los Angeles—Roy McDonald Assoc., Inc.
Wheeling (Chicago)—David A. Hanley & Associates.
New York—Alliance Publishers Representatives.

**3. COMMISSION AND CASH DISCOUNT**
15% to recognized agencies with satisfactory credit rating, on space, bleed, and position only, if paid within 30 days of billing date.

**4. GENERAL RATE POLICY**
All rates subject to change upon 60 days notice.

**ADVERTISING RATES**
Effective January 01, 1990. (issue) (Card No. 25)
Rates received October 12, 1989.

**5. BLACK/WHITE RATES**

| | 1 ti | 3 ti | 6 ti | 12 ti | 18 ti | 24 ti |
|---|---|---|---|---|---|---|
| 1 page | 2700. | 2480. | 2260. | 2040. | 1820. | 1600. |
| 2/3 page | 2105. | 1910. | 1715. | 1520. | ... | ... |
| 1/2 page | 1760. | 1580. | 1400. | 1220. | ... | ... |
| 1/3 page | 1280. | 1130. | 980. | 830. | ... | ... |
| 1/4 page | 990. | 880. | 770. | 660. | ... | ... |
| 1/6 page | 580. | 520. | 460. | 400. | ... | ... |
| 1 inch | 260. | 240. | 220. | 200. | ... | ... |

**6. COLOR RATES**
Standard AAAA colors, blue or yellow, extra ............ 435.
All other standard AAAA colors or matched colors, extra ............ 540.
3 or 4 color process, extra ............ 930.

**8. INSERTS**
Black and white page rates apply.
Back-up charges and tip-in charges available.

**9. BLEED**
Extra ............ 15%

**10. SPECIAL POSITION**
Extra ............ 10%

**11. CLASSIFIED/MAIL ORDER/SPECIALTY RATES**
DISPLAY CLASSIFICATIONS:
MOTOR COACH MART
For the buying and selling of motor coaches and supplies. .50 per word for running copy. Minimum 10 words. Display Classified ads are 8.00 per line. Payment in advance. No agency commission. Ads must be received in writing.
MAIL ORDER MART

| | 1 ti | 3 ti | 6 ti | 12 ti |
|---|---|---|---|---|
| 1/9 page | 115. | 110. | 105. | 100. |

No agency commission.

**15. MECH. REQUIREMENTS**
**Also see SRDS Print Media Production Data.**
Printing Process: Web Offset.
Trim size: 8-1/8 x 10-7/8; No./Cols. 2&3.
Binding method: Perfect.
Colors Available: AAAA/ABP; Matched; 4-color Process (AAAA/MPA).

DIMENSIONS-AD PAGE

| | | | |
|---|---|---|---|
| 1 | 7 x 10 | 1/4 | 4-9/16 x 3-3/4 |
| 2/3 | 4-9/16 x 10 | 1/4 | 7 x 2-3/8 |
| 1/2 | 4-9/16 x 7-1/2 | 1/6 | 2-3/16 x 4-7/8 |
| 1/2 | 7 x 5 | 1/6 | 4-9/16 x 2-3/8 |
| 1/3 | 2-3/16 x 10 | 1" | 2-3/16 x 1 |
| 1/3 | 4-9/16 x 5 | | |

**16. ISSUE AND CLOSING DATES**
Published monthly.

| Issue: | On sale | Closing | Issue: | On sale | Closing |
|---|---|---|---|---|---|
| Jan | ... | 11/15 | Jul | ... | 5/15 |
| Feb | ... | 12/15 | Aug | ... | 6/15 |
| Mar | ... | 1/15 | Sep | ... | 7/15 |
| Apr | ... | 2/15 | Oct | ... | 8/15 |
| May | ... | 3/15 | Nov | ... | 9/15 |
| Jun | ... | 4/15 | Dec | ... | 10/15 |

No cancellations accepted after closing.

**18. CIRCULATION**
Established 1964. Single copy 2.50; per year 20.00.
**SWORN 12-31-89 (6 mos. aver.)**

| Total | Non-paid | Paid | (Subs.) | (Single) | [Assoc.] |
|---|---|---|---|---|---|
| 85,000 | 3,642 | 81,358 | 81,358 | ... | 81,358 |

(C-B)

### Good Sam's HI-WAY HERALD
**A TL Enterprises, Inc. Publication**

Media Code 8 135 3250 4.00 — Mid 000223-000

Published monthly by TL Enterprises, Inc., 29901 Agoura Road, Agoura, CA 91301. Phone 818-991-4980.

**PUBLISHER'S EDITORIAL PROFILE**

GOOD SAM'S HI-WAY HERALD contains news articles on matters of interest to the members of Good Sam Recreational Vehicle Owners Club, as reflecting state and national news which may affect their lives, as well as former and upcoming club functions. In a year, the editorial content covers national club matters 25%, local and regional club items of interest 50%, opinion (mail from members) 10% and topics 15%. Rec'd 4/16/79.

**1. PERSONNEL**
Editor—Beverly Edwards.
Advertising Director—Chuck Kastler.

**2. REPRESENTATIVES and/or BRANCH OFFICES**
Elkhart 46516—Janet VanBibber, Mike Brazeau, James Paxton, Thomas Smith, Jim Mac, Fred Schwartz, Peg Recchio, Adv. Sales, Tom Bittle, General Manager Midwest/East Operations, 2300 Middlebury St. Phone 219-295-7820.
Agoura, CA 91301—K. Dale Mattox, Ralph Kelsey, Dan Seidlitz, P.O. Box 5500. Phone 818-991-4980.
Selingsgrove, PA—Frank Ryan Associates (Mail Order).

**3. COMMISSION AND CASH DISCOUNT**
15% to recognized agencies. 2% 10 days of invoice. Net 30 days.

**ADVERTISING RATES**
Effective October, 1989. (issue)
Rates received May 24, 1989.

**5. BLACK/WHITE RATES**

| | 1 ti | 6 ti | 12 ti | 24 ti | 36 ti | 48 ti |
|---|---|---|---|---|---|---|
| 1 page | 10,265. | 9,735. | 8,320. | 7,655. | 7,440. | 7,090. |
| 2/3 page | 7,635. | 7,085. | 6,195. | 5,725. | 5,540. | 5,205. |
| 1/2 page | 5,985. | 5,515. | 4,795. | 4,380. | 4,210. | 4,085. |
| 1/3 page | 4,145. | 3,760. | 3,260. | 2,975. | 2,850. | 2,815. |
| 1/4 page | 3,075. | 2,795. | 2,405. | 2,190. | 2,055. | 2,010. |
| 1/6 page | 2,110. | 1,915. | 1,635. | 1,485. | 1,440. | 1,390. |
| 1/8 page | 1,705. | 1,615. | 1,385. | 1,270. | 1,225. | 1,190. |
| 1/12 page | 1,260. | 1,205. | 1,030. | 945. | 915. | 870. |
| 1 inch | 590. | ... | ... | ... | ... | ... |

CONTINUITY RATES
One full page or more in 12 consecutive issues in Hi-Way Herald.

| | | | |
|---|---|---|---|
| 12 pages | 8115. | 60 pages | 6775. |
| 24 pages | 7455. | 72 pages | 6555. |
| 36 pages | 7245. | 84 pages | 6375. |
| 48 pages | 6890. | 96 pages | 6190. |

**5a. COMBINATION RATES**
Space contracted for in Trailer Life Publications can be combined to earn lowest possible frequency rate in each publication.

**6. COLOR RATES**
2 color:

| | 1 ti | 6 ti | 12 ti | 24 ti | 36 ti |
|---|---|---|---|---|---|
| 1 page | 10,965. | 10,445. | 9,025. | 8,360. | 8,150. |
| 2/3 page | 8,435. | 7,810. | 6,905. | 6,430. | 6,245. |
| 1/2 page | 6,695. | 6,225. | 5,510. | 5,090. | 4,910. |
| 1/3 page | 4,850. | 4,470. | 3,970. | 3,685 | 3,560. |

| | 48 ti |
|---|---|
| 1 page | 7,805. |
| 2/3 page | 5,915. |
| 1/2 page | 4,790. |
| 1/3 page | 3,520. |

4 color:

| | | | | | |
|---|---|---|---|---|---|
| 1 page | 14,845. | 14,085. | 12,030. | 11,070. | 10,760. |
| 2/3 page | 12,175. | 11,550. | 9,895. | 9,140. | 8,840. |
| 1/2 page | 10,150. | 9,355. | 8,140. | 7,425. | 7,130. |
| 1/3 page | 7,665. | 6,965. | 6,040. | 5,500. | 5,270. |

| | |
|---|---|
| 1 page | 10,260. |
| 2/3 page | 8,300. |
| 1/2 page | 6,920. |
| 1/3 page | 5,210. |

CONTINUITY RATES
One full page or more in 12 consecutive issues in Hi-Way Herald.

| | 2 color | 4 color | | 2 color | 4 color |
|---|---|---|---|---|---|
| 12 pages | 8,830. | 11,830. | 60 pages | 7,490. | 10,060. |
| 24 pages | 8,160. | 10,900. | 72 pages | 7,265. | 9,845. |
| 36 pages | 7,950. | 10,645. | 84 pages | 7,085. | 9,690. |
| 48 pages | 7,600. | 10,170. | 96 pages | 6,895. | 9,565. |

**7. COVERS**
4 color:

| | 1 ti | 6 ti | 12 ti |
|---|---|---|---|
| 2nd cover | 17,815. | 16,900. | 14,430. |
| 3rd cover | 17,070. | 16,200. | 13,835. |
| 4th cover | 18,555. | 17,605. | 15,035. |

**8. INSERTS**
Available.

**11. CLASSIFIED/MAIL ORDER/SPECIALTY RATES**
CLASSIFIED:
Commercial Corner-30.00/line, 5-line minimum. 6 issues-5%; 12 issues-10%.
DISPLAY CLASSIFICATIONS:
RV MARKETPLACE

| | 1 ti | 6 ti | 12 ti | | 1 ti | 6 ti | 12 ti |
|---|---|---|---|---|---|---|---|
| 1 inch | 405. | 305. | 215. | 3 inches | 680. | 585. | 480. |
| 2 inches | 540. | 445. | 345. | | | | |

CAMPGROUND AND RV PARK SECTION

| | 3 ti | 6 ti | 12 ti | | 3 ti | 6 ti | 12 ti |
|---|---|---|---|---|---|---|---|
| 1 inch | 370. | 275. | 195. | 3 inches | 620. | 530. | 435. |
| 2 inches | 490. | 405. | 315. | | | | |

**13a. GEOGRAPHIC and/or DEMOGRAPHIC EDITIONS**

REGION 1-NORTHWEST
Includes Alaska, Idaho, Montana, Oregon, Washington, Wyoming, Western Canada.
BLACK AND WHITE RATES:

| | 1 ti | 6 ti | 12 ti | 24 ti | 36 ti | 48 ti |
|---|---|---|---|---|---|---|
| 1 page | 2185. | 1940. | 1715. | 1610. | 1580. | 1520. |
| 2/3 page | 1670. | 1500. | 1355. | 1260. | 1225. | 1185. |
| 1/2 page | 1285. | 1145. | 1040. | 985. | 970. | 935. |
| 1/3 page | 910. | 830. | 720. | 670. | 660. | 640. |
| 1/4 page | 705. | 630. | 555. | 520. | 510. | 495. |
| 1/6 page | 535. | 475. | 420. | 390. | 385. | 375. |

CIRCULATION:
Publisher states: "Effective with October 1988 issue, rates based on a circulation average of 75,400."

REGION 2-SOUTHWEST
Includes Arizona, California, Colorado, Hawaii, Nevada, New Mexico, Utah.
BLACK AND WHITE RATES:

| | 1 ti | 6 ti | 12 ti | 24 ti | 36 ti | 48 ti |
|---|---|---|---|---|---|---|
| 1 page | 5000. | 4395. | 3805. | 3540. | 3445. | 3300. |
| 2/3 page | 3800. | 3280. | 2905. | 2705. | 2640. | 2490. |
| 1/2 page | 3045. | 2615. | 2310. | 2145. | 2070. | 2010. |
| 1/3 page | 2035. | 1780. | 1555. | 1445. | 1410. | 1345. |
| 1/4 page | 1545. | 1355. | 1185. | 1100. | 1075. | 1035. |
| 1/6 page | 1105. | 990. | 840. | 755. | 745. | 725. |

CIRCULATION:
Publisher states: "Effective with october 1988 issue, rates based on a circulation average of 260,800."

REGION 3&4-MIDWEST/CENTRAL
Includes Arkansa, Illinois, Iowa, Kansas, Louisiana, Minnesota, Missouri, Nebraska, North Dakota, Oklahoma, South Dakota, Texas, Wisconsin.
BLACK AND WHITE RATES:

| | 1 ti | 6 ti | 12 ti | 24 ti | 36 ti | 48 ti |
|---|---|---|---|---|---|---|
| 1 page | 3180. | 2810. | 2455. | 2285. | 2235. | 2155. |
| 2/3 page | 2430. | 2140. | 1880. | 1760. | 1725. | 1650. |
| 1/2 page | 1965. | 1710. | 1505. | 1400. | 1370. | 1350. |
| 1/3 page | 1315. | 1105. | 1010. | 945. | 920. | 895. |
| 1/4 page | 995. | 880. | 765. | 715. | 700. | 680. |
| 1/6 page | 730. | 625. | 560. | 515. | 505. | 485. |

CIRCULATION:
Publisher states: "Effective with October 1988 issue, rates based on a circulation average of 136,200."

REGION 5-NORTHEAST
Includes Connecticut, Indiana, Maine, Massachusetts, Michigan, New Hampshire, New Jersey, New York, Ohio, Pennsylvania, Rhode Island, Vermont, Eastern Canada.
BLACK AND WHITE RATES

| | 1 ti | 6 ti | 12 ti | 24 ti | 36 ti | 48 ti |
|---|---|---|---|---|---|---|
| 1 page | 2945. | 2605. | 2270. | 2115. | 2005. | 1980. |
| 2/3 page | 2255. | 1965. | 1750. | 1635. | 1590. | 1520. |
| 1/2 page | 1830. | 1590. | 1430. | 1360. | 1280. | 1250. |
| 1/3 page | 1225. | 1070. | 945. | 880. | 835. | 815. |
| 1/4 page | 935. | 810. | 720. | 670. | 635. | 620. |
| 1/6 page | 680. | 585. | 515. | 470. | 460. | 455. |

CIRCULATION:
Publisher states: "Effective with October 1988 issue, rates based on a circulation average of 120,800."

REGION 6-SOUTHEAST
Includes Alabama, Delaware, District of Columbia, Florida, Georgia, Kentucky, Maryland, Mississippi, North Carolina, South Carolina, Tennessee, Virginia, West Virginia.
BLACK AND WHITE RATES

| | 1 ti | 6 ti | 12 ti | 24 ti | 36 ti | 48 ti |
|---|---|---|---|---|---|---|
| 1 page | 2710. | 2400. | 2100. | 1975. | 1940. | 1860. |
| 2/3 page | 2105. | 1830. | 1640. | 1535. | 1505. | 1440. |
| 1/2 page | 1680. | 1515. | 1330. | 1260. | 1210. | 1175. |
| 1/3 page | 1145. | 1005. | 895. | 825. | 810. | 790. |
| 1/4 page | 880. | 775. | 675. | 640. | 625. | 600. |
| 1/6 page | 650. | 555. | 510. | 475. | 465. | 450. |

CIRCULATION:
Publisher states: "Effective with October 1988 issue, rates based on circulation average of 106,800."

**14. CONTRACT AND COPY REGULATIONS**
See Contents page for location—items 1, 2, 12, 17, 24, 27, 30, 32, 35, 42.

**15. MECH. REQUIREMENTS**
**Also see SRDS Print Media Production Data.**
Printing Process: Web Offset.
Trim size: 10-3/4 x 8; No./Cols. 3.
Binding method: Saddle-stitch.
Colors available: Publisher's Standard; 4-color process (AAAA/MPA).

DIMENSIONS-AD PAGE

| | | | |
|---|---|---|---|
| 1 | 7-1/4 x 10 | 1/6 | 2-1/4 x 4-7/8 |
| 2/3 | 4-3/4 x 10 | 1/6 | 4-3/4 x 2-3/8 |
| 1/2 | 4-3/4 x 7-3/8 | 1/8 | 2-1/4 x 3-1/2 |
| 1/2 | 7-1/4 x 4-7/8 | 1/9 | 2-1/4 x 2-7/8 |
| 1/3 | 2-1/4 x 10 | 1/12 | 2-1/4 x 2-1/4 |
| 1/3 | 4-3/4 x 4-7/8 | Col. in. | 2-1/4 x 1 |
| 1/4 | 4-3/4 x 3-5/8 | | |

**16. ISSUE AND CLOSING DATES**
Published monthly.

| Issue: | Closing Space Reserv. | Film | Mailing |
|---|---|---|---|
| October/89 | 8/4 | 8/9 | 9/7 |
| November/89 | 9/6 | 9/11 | 10/10 |
| December/89 | 10/5 | 10/10 | 11/8 |
| January/90 | 11/3 | 11/8 | 12/11 |
| February/90 | 12/5 | 12/8 | 1/10 |
| March/90 | 1/4 | 1/9 | 2/7 |
| April/90 | 2/5 | 2/8 | 3/12 |
| May/90 | 3/5 | 3/8 | 4/6 |
| June/90 | 4/3 | 4/6 | 5/7 |
| July/90 | 5/3 | 5/8 | 6/7 |
| August/90 | 6/5 | 6/8 | 7/9 |
| September/90 | 7/6 | 7/11 | 8/9 |

Ads that require production and non-camera-ready material must be submitted by the issue's closing date for space reservations. Cancellations cannot be executed after the closing date unless authorized by publisher. If new material for contracted scheduled insertion is not received by closing date, publisher reserves the right to repeat the most recent insertion.

**18. CIRCULATION**
Established 1967. Single copy .50; per year 6.00
**SWORN 6-30-89 (6 mos. aver.)**

| Total | Non-Pd | Paid | (Subs) | (Single) | [Assoc] |
|---|---|---|---|---|---|
| 671,512 | 38,918 | 632,594 | 632,594 | ... | 632,594 |

Unpaid Distribution (not incl. above):
Total 6,215
TERRITORIAL DISTRIBUTION 6/89—678,324

| N.Eng. | Mid.Atl. | E.N.Cen. | W.N.Cen. | S.Atl. | E.S.Cen. |
|---|---|---|---|---|---|
| 25,780 | 41,520 | 73,755 | 43,173 | 82,474 | 19,039 |
| W.S.Cen. | Mtn.St. | Pac.St. | Canada | Foreign | Other |
| 63,592 | 78,610 | 240,509 | 9,681 | 159 | 23 |

(C-C3)

### MOTORHOME
**A TL Er ...ises, Inc. Publication**

The Audit Bureau

Media Code 8 135 4 ... 00 — Mid 000212-000

Published 12 tim... year by TL Enterprises, Inc., ...Phone 818-991-

**CIRCULATION**

...OFILE
...for owners and ...vacation vehicles. Editorial material is both technical and non-technical in nature. Regular features include tests and descriptions of various models of motorhomes and mini-motorhomes, travel adventures on such vehicles, and objective analysis of equipment and supplies for such self-propelled recreational vehicles. Guides and directories within the magazine provide listings of manufacturers, rentals and other sources of equipment and accessories of interest to enthusiasts. Rec'd 11/28/77.

**1. PERSONNEL**
Editor—Bob Livingston.
Publisher—Rick Rouse.
Associate Publisher—Bill Estes.
Advertising Director—Chuck Kastler.

**2. REPRESENTATIVES and/or BRANCH OFFICES**
Agoura, CA 91301—K. Dale Mattox, Ralph Kelsey, Dan Seidlitz, Advertising Sales, P.O. Box 5500. Phone 818-991-4980.
Elkhart, IN 46516—Tom Bittle, General Manager, Midwest/East Operations, Mike Brazeau, Janet VanBibber, Peg Recchio, Advertising Sales, 2300 Middlebury. Phone 219-295-7820. Jim Mac; Phone 800-423-4231, ext. 75589.
Selinsgrove, PA—Frank Ryan Associates (Mail Order).

**3. COMMISSION AND CASH DISCOUNT**
15% to recognized agencies. 2% cash discount if paid within 10 days.

**ADVERTISING RATES**
Effective October, 1989. (issue)
Rates received May 24, 1989.

**5. BLACK/WHITE RATES**

| | 1 ti | 6 ti | 12 ti | 24 ti | 36 ti | 48 ti |
|---|---|---|---|---|---|---|
| 1 page | 4405. | 4110. | 3595. | 3285. | 3195. | 3065. |
| 2/3 page | 3280. | 3040. | 2650. | 2445. | 2370. | 2285. |
| 1/2 page | 2635. | 2460. | 2120. | 1965. | 1915. | 1830. |
| 1/3 page | 1775. | 1660. | 1450. | 1325. | 1290. | 1235. |
| 1/4 page | 1355. | 1260. | 1085. | 1010. | 980. | 945. |
| 1/6 page | 1090. | 1005. | 870. | 805. | 780. | 750. |
| Column inch | 420. | ... | ... | ... | ... | ... |

Minimum rateholder 1/6 page.
Frequency rates based on times run within a 12-month period.

CONTINUITY RATES
1 page or more in 12 consecutive issues.

| | | | |
|---|---|---|---|
| 12 pages | 3490. | 60 pages | 2925. |
| 24 pages | 3270. | 72 pages | 2890. |
| 36 pages | 3100. | 84 pages | 2850. |
| 48 pages | 2965. | 96 pages | 2825. |

**5a. COMBINATION RATES**
Similar size insertions in Motorhome and any other TL Enterprises publication can be combined to earn the lowest possible frequency rate in each publication.

**6. COLOR RATES**
2 color:

| | 1 ti | 6 ti | 12 ti | 24 ti | 36 ti | 48 ti |
|---|---|---|---|---|---|---|
| 1 page | 5245. | 4930. | 4420. | 4105. | 3945. | 3845. |
| 2/3 page | 4065. | 3820. | 3385. | 3185. | 3065. | 2985. |
| 1/2 page | 3415. | 3245. | 2850. | 2675. | 2575. | 2505. |
| 1/3 page | 2740. | 2580. | 2315. | 2055. | 1965. | 1665. |

4 color:

| | 1 ti | 6 ti | 12 ti | 24 ti | 36 ti | 48 ti |
|---|---|---|---|---|---|---|
| 1 page | 6325. | 5860. | 5225. | 4920. | 4720. | 4600. |
| 2/3 page | 5045. | 4675. | 4190. | 3910. | 3805. | 3690. |
| 1/2 page | 4205. | 3905. | 3475. | 3310. | 3230. | 3120. |
| 1/3 page | 3345. | 3130. | 2820. | 2625. | 2570. | 2490. |

CONTINUITY RATES
1 page or more in 12 consecutive issues.

| | 2 color | 4 color | | 2 color | 4 color |
|---|---|---|---|---|---|
| 12 pages | 4285. | 5145. | 60 pages | 3570. | 4385. |
| 24 pages | 4020. | 4870. | 72 pages | 3515. | 4320. |
| 36 pages | 3805. | 4645. | 84 pages | 3455. | 4250. |
| 48 pages | 3640. | 4470. | 96 pages | 3415. | 4200. |

**7. COVERS**

| | 1 ti | 6 ti | 12 ti |
|---|---|---|---|
| 2nd cover (4 color) | 7590. | 7030. | 6275. |
| 3rd cover (4 color) | 7275. | 6740. | 6010. |
| 4th cover (4 color) | 8410. | 7790. | 6950. |

**8. INSERTS**
Available.

**9. BLEED**
Extra ............ 10%

**10. SPECIAL POSITION**
Extra ............ 10%

## *Your National Association*

The National Campground Owners' Association (NCOA) collects many types of information about the camping industry. One valuable report is the Campground Industry National Economic Survey & Analysis, which shows campground use by state or region. This report and other potentially valuable statistics are available upon request by writing to

NCOA
11307 Sunset Hills Rd.
Suite B-7
Reston, VA 22090.

Take advantage of all this research to refine your definition of your own customer. This is the most critical knowledge you can gather for your marketing plan. Knowing your customer is the secret to making all the other steps work, and you can never learn too much. The more you know, the less it will cost for you to reach the right people with promotions and messages about your campground — and the less money you'll spend talking to people who don't fit your customer definition.

How do you make sense out of all the data and statistics you have collected? Relate it back to your definition of your customer. You can begin to see the importance of knowing not only who your customers are, but also how many of them there are, where they are traveling, what they spend, what activities they're most interested in, and what they're planning for the future. This is the first and most important step in promoting your campground and increasing your profits.

# STEP 2: ANALYZING THE COMPETITION

Now that you know who your customers are, the next step is finding out who your competitors are and what they're offering. The steps described here will show you an easy, inexpensive way to get this information and use it in your plan.

Select as many competitors as you can find. Consult NCOA's industry report, local business listings and ads in camping magazines to find out who your competitors are.

The key to collecting information is to put yourself into the role of an individual customer. If you want to know more about your competitors for RV customers, for instance, make your inquiries as if you were an RV owner.

Ask about only one type of facility at a time. A true customer is interested in only the type of camping facility that corresponds to the camper he or she owns.

Read your competitors' ads and send for any information they offer by mail. Use your home address & phone — not your campground address. Or send a letter identifying your camping interest ("I have a recreational vehicle...") and requesting information ("I'm interested in the rates and types of facilities at your campground....").

The brochures and written responses you get will show you how other campgrounds are marketing their services and will help you determine just who your competitors really are. If you're trying to attract RV owners, for example, a campground that doesn't offer RV parking isn't really a true competitor.

Narrow down your list and begin filling out the Competitor Analysis Form included here. Spend some time analyzing the written information, and summarize it on the form for future use.

Some questions to get you started:

- What type of literature did they send you — color brochure, personal letter, reservation form, flyers on local attractions, etc.?

- How quickly did they respond? — A speedy response may give you an indication of which campgrounds are really "on the ball."
- What are their prices? Are yours competitive?
- Was there a follow-up mailing? What did it include?
- What campground features are they stressing — physical layout, price, service, locations, etc.?
- How are they saying it? — The copy and the look of their brochures will give you an idea of the "image" the campground is trying to promote.
- What advantages do they have over your campground?
- What disadvantages do you see?
- Does the literature information correspond to the competitor's magazine advertising? — Note any discrepancies.

After you get the brochure or written response, call the campground and ask them the same questions you asked them by mail. Use the form to record what you learn. Keep track of what they're telling you in the mail and on the telephone, and compare it. What you want to know is whether or not they're saying the same thing. If there's a difference, you may be able to use that to your advantage.

For example, if a competitor's ads or brochures say the campground offers a boat launch, call the campground and ask specific questions about these facilities. If the staff tells you that the facilities are in fact three miles away at the public landing, then you've found a discrepancy. That campground's customers — the same ones you're competing for — may well be disappointed and look for more convenient boating facilities the next time they camp. If your campground has an advantage, you now know the value of stressing it in your own promotions and advertising.

| COMPETITOR ANALYSIS FORM | | | | |
|---|---|---|---|---|
| | DATE RECEIVED | | MATERIALS RECEIVED | |
| CAMPGROUND | P | B | PERSONAL INQUIRY | BINGO |
| | | | | |
| | | | | |
| | | | | |
| | | | | |
| | | | | |

# STEP 3: EVALUATING YOUR PRODUCT

The final step in developing your initial marketing plan is one that is missed by many business owners, especially those who don't have a marketing or advertising background.

Evaluating your product is an important step in understanding how your potential customers perceive what you have to offer.

This involves more than just walking around your campground and making sure that the grass is mowed and the plumbing works. In marketing, evaluating the product means looking at it from the standpoint of your defined customer. You need information from both your current and potential customers. Current users can give you detailed information about what they feel are your campground's strengths and weaknesses. Potential customers — those who haven't yet visited your campground — can tell you what they know about your facilities and how they're responding to the promotions and messages you're directing to them.

You can collect this information by having your current and potential customers provide answers to a few simple questions. Use the Product Evaluation form included here as a guide for developing your own questionnaire.

The very first question that must be asked and answered is this: Did you understand the features and benefits being offered by my campground? To do this, give one of your potential customers a piece of your literature, a copy of your ad, or anything you're using to promote your campground. Ask whether he or she 1) understands what you're offering, and 2) how to become one of your customers. Also ask whether this camper has any unanswered questions.

Then find out what your potential customer likes about your campground. Ask which features are of the most interest and which ones he or she would consider to be disadvantages. Then ask whether or not this camper would like to use the campground, how often, and at what cost.

Give your questionnaire to several potential customers, and keep track of the results. Then collect the same type of information from current campers who match your targeted customer group. From the responses, you'll see what customers believe the weak areas of your product might be. You can then take steps to remedy these before you begin full-scale promotional activities for your campground.

### PRODUCT EVALUATION FORM

**TYPE OF CAMPER:** _____

[ ] Current Customer          [ ] Potential Customer

**QUESTIONS:**

1. Do you understand the main features and benefits being offered by the ABC campground?

    [ ] Yes    [ ] No

2. Which features of the campground are most beneficial to you?

    _____
    _____
    _____
    _____

3. What campground features do you consider to be disadvantages?

    _____
    _____

4. Based on what you know about the ABC Campground, would you consider staying at ABC?

    [ ] Yes    [ ] No    *(If YES, please answer Question 5)*

5. If you would be interested in camping at ABC, when would you be most likely to use the campground?

    [ ] Summer vacation
    [ ] Other: _____
    [ ] Weekend getaway    [ ] Weekdays

    How often would you use the campground?

        [ ] Once a year    [ ] Twice a year    [ ] Three times a year or more

    How long would your stay be?

        [ ] One night only    [ ] 2 to 3 nights    [ ] 4 nights or more

# STEP 4: PUTTING IT ALL TOGETHER

Now look at everything you've collected.

You've decided who is most likely to use your campground. You know how many potential customers you have. You know what type of camping equipment they're using. You know where they're living, what they're interested in, how often they camp. You know what they're reading and the type of messages they're getting from your competitors. You know where you stand in the camping market — you've compared your campground to competing campgrounds, and you know your advantages and disadvantages from your defined customer's point of view.

Summarize this information on the Analysis Form provided here and look at what you have. Your goal is to come up with a "Common Denominator" — the one key feature, benefit or advantage that you can use to promote your campground to the specific customer you have defined. This is the heart of your marketing plan and the secret to its success.

Once you get this system working for you, it will continue to provide you with profitable information as long as you're in business. You can set goals, keep track of your success and easily adapt your plan from year to year. If your business environment changes, your existing plan will help you redefine your customer and your campground's competitive advantages and disadvantages. Whatever happens, you'll have a system for finding out what affects you and how you can respond to it.

## ANALYSIS FORM

**DESCRIBE CUSTOMERS:**

| | CAMPER TYPE | HOW MANY | DISTANCE TRAVELED |
|---|---|---|---|
| 1. | | | |
| 2. | | | |
| 3. | | | |
| 4. | | | |

**DESCRIBE COMPETITOR:**

| | CAMPER TYPE | NUMBER UNITS | PRICE RANGE |
|---|---|---|---|
| 1. | | | |
| 2. | | | |
| 3. | | | |
| 4. | | | |

**COMMON DENOMINATORS:** _____

_____

_____

_____

_____

# 2    PLANNING FOR THE FUTURE: SETTING THE BUDGET

All successful businesses set goals or objectives to guide their business activities. These goals are more than just hoped-for results; these goals give you a framework for making all your business decisions and show you the direction in which you're going. And once you get there, they let you know you're arriving.

Setting goals is especially important when you're deciding on your budget for marketing. Unlike salaries, loan payments, utilities and other fixed costs, the amount you spend on marketing can vary widely depending on the decisions you make about its impor-

tance. The results of a wrong decision can be expensive. If you don't allocate enough to marketing, the little you do spend won't do the work it was designed to do. And if you spend too much, you'll be wasting your profits.

By specifically defining your marketing goals, you can avoid this guesswork and build success into your marketing plan. This chapter shows you how to set your goals and use them to guide all your budgeting activities.

# STEP 1: SETTING YOUR MARKETING GOALS

There are two types of goals you will be setting for your campground business in general:

1. Short-term goals — realistically what can be met in a relatively short period of time, usually a year or less.
   Examples of short-term goals would be

   - To decrease the vacancy rate by X%
   - To increase site rentals by X%
   - To make a physical improvement to the camp sites
   - To offer a new service

2. Long-term goals — specifically what you want to do and where you want your campground to be in one to five years.
   Examples of long-term goals would be

   - To make major physical improvements to the campground
   - To offer incentives for increasing weekday business
   - To expand facilities or acquire new land
   - To establish a regional or national reputation

Use the Goal Setting form provided and think about all the possible improvements in facilities, services, sales and profits you want to make in the next five years. Decide on the most important ones that realistically can be accomplished in the indicated periods of time. Then write them down on the form so you have a record of your decisions.

Use a separate form for each of the specific customers you defined in the last chapter. Consider all the activities you might undertake and the improvements you could make to increase your sales to each type of customer. Consider one customer category at a time and decide on what you can do in the next year (short-term goals) and what you want to accomplish eventually (long-term goals).

EXAMPLE: You have defined recreational vehicle owners as the main type of customer you want to attract. Possible short-term goals for that customer might be

- To begin advertising in recreational vehicle magazines
- To repair and refurbish RV pads
- To stock and sell RV supplies in my campground store

Possible long-term goals for your RV customer might be

- To increase national consumer awareness of my campground among RV owners
- To add ten new RV pads
- To establish a national or regional reputation as a top RV camp site

## GOAL SETTING FORM

TYPE OF DEFINED CUSTOMER: _____

CAMPGROUND LOCATION: _____

_____

SHORT-TERM GOALS:

1. _____

2. _____

3. _____

4. _____

LONG-TERM GOALS:

1. _____

2. _____

3. _____

4. _____

## STEP 2: FORECASTING

### Refining Your Goals

You now need to determine whether or not the goals you have set are attainable. Are they realistic? Can you accomplish them with the resources you have? Does the local, regional or national campground market offer the potential for you to "fit in" the way you want?

You'll find most of the answers to these questions in the customer and competitor research you did in Chapter One. Go back to the packages of information you collected from the camping magazines, NCOA, trade associations, industry and government reports and other sources. Go through them and jot down information about the general camping market and the specific markets for your defined customers. The major information you want to record and organize includes

• Past sales patterns of the entire campground industry   $_____/_____

• General industry trends and growth   _____

• Average sales and spending for individual campgrounds of various sizes   $_____/_____

• Your direct competitors' sales patterns and spending   $_____/_____

• Past sales patterns for specific customer groups   $_____

• The total amount spent on camping by each customer group   $_____

• Economic conditions and trends   _____

Next, look at your campground's own business information and the goals you've just set. Write down all the data that corresponds to the categories of information you collected for the campground industry above. You'll want to include

• Your campground's past sales patterns and rate of growth   $_____/_____%

• Your campground's projected sales patterns   $_____

• The short-term and long-term sales goals you've set   $_____/_____

Now compare the two sets of figures to determine how closely your goals and projections match that of what the market offers. Look at the spending and sales data for campgrounds the same size as yours and for your direct competitors. Some questions to answer:

- Are your campground's current and projected sales similar to those of other campgrounds of your size or in your region?

- Are your goals set far higher or lower than the industry averages?

- Are there any major differences in your product (facilities, prices, services or location) that justify the differences?

- Do the industry's projected sales trends match the rate of growth your goals call for?

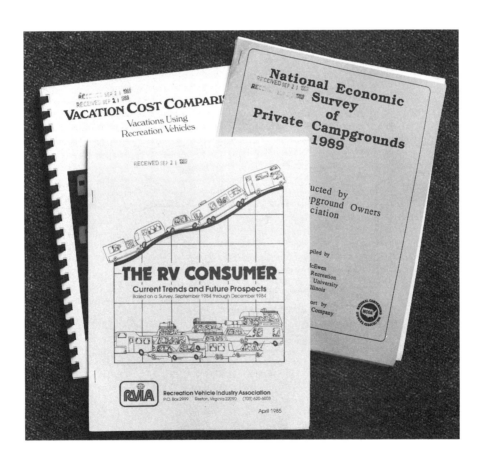

## Using the Forecasting Form

After making comparisons between your campground and the industry as a whole, you may want to modify your goals. Make those changes on the Goal Setting form and then fill out the Forecasting form. Use the data you've organized to answer the specific questions on the form — it will lead you to the conclusions you need to make in forecasting your own campground's sales and growth.

## FORECASTING FORM

### LAST YEAR

Number of units rented                    _____
    (One day's rental of one site is a unit.
    Total units rented is the number of
    campsites multiplied by the total number
    of days each was rented)

Number of weekend days campsites were
    rented                                _____
    (Number of campsites multiplied by
    the number of weekend days they were
    filled)

Number of weekdays campsites were
    rented                                _____
    (Number of campsites multiplied by
    the number of weekdays they were
    filled)

### NEXT YEAR

Total possible rentals                    _____
    (Add up the total number of calendar
    days your campground is open during
    the year by the number of campsites)

Number of possible weekend day
    rentals                               _____
    (Count the number of weekend days
    during the campground season and
    multiply by the number of campsites
    you have available)

Number of possible weekday
    rentals                               _____
    (Count the number of weekdays
    during the campground season and
    multiply by the number of campsites
    you have available)

Number of units expected to rent    _____
    (From the Goal Setting form)

Price that can be charged per unit    _____
    (Use competitor averages and industry
    trends to figure a reasonable site rental
    fee for next season)

## Your Own Campground's Sales Forecast

At this point in the forecasting process, you've set your own short-term and long-term goals, you've analyzed the marketplace, and you have a good idea that your goals are realistic and attainable. You're now ready to put your goals to work by applying some real-world numbers.

To begin the forecasting process for your own campground business, you'll need good figures from your business records. The process involves using a cost accounting method to break down your income and expenses. Whatever type of bookkeeping or accounting system you use, go through your records and write down the last full year's totals for your campground business only. *If you have a retail store or other auxiliary business on site, those costs and expenses should be separated from the figures for the actual campground use.*

For quick reference later in this chapter, use the form below to record totals for the following categories:

Total revenues (income) from actual campground rentals _ _ _ _ _ _ _ _ _ _ _ _ _ _ _ _$_____

Fixed expenses: the overhead costs of running your campground whether or not you rent any of the campsites. (Fixed expenses include, but are not limited to, salaries, insurance, utilities, property taxes, interest on loans, purchased goods & supplies, purchased services, licensing fees, etc.)  _ _ _ _ _ _ _ _ _ _ _ _ _ _ _$_____

Variable expenses: the extra expenses you incur when a campsite is being used. (These might include extra utility usage, garbage pick-up, maintenance & repair costs, the cost of extra services you provide, etc.) If these variable costs are very low, they may be insignificant in the budgeting process._ _ _ _ _ _ _ _ _ _ _ _ _$_____

Total spent on advertising, promotions and other marketing activities last year _ _ _ _ _$_____

TOTAL EXPENSES _ _ _ _ _ _ _ _ _ _ _ _ _ _ _ _ _ _ _ _ _ _ _ _ _ _ _$_____

A marketing forecast deals only with your actual sales, not with your profit margin. Marketing itself is concerned with selling a certain number of units at a given price. Profit is a function of management. The key to making your budgeting system work is to consider marketing costs first and then your profit margin. Many business owners make the mistake of figuring the profit they need and then using what's "left over" to market the product. The system here will help you avoid this pitfall — it builds the cost of marketing into the price you charge.

**EXAMPLE**: The campground is open from April 15 until September 30 (168 days: 50 weekend days; 118 weekdays) and has 200 available sites.

|  LAST YEAR  |  NEXT YEAR  |

Number of units rented: 13,500
(150 sites x 90 days)

Number of weekend days campsites were rented: 7,500
(150 sites x 50 nights)

Number of weekdays campsites were rented: 6,000
(100 sites x 60 nights)

Total possible rentals: 33,600
(200 sites x 168 days)

Number of possible weekend day rentals: 10,000
(200 sites x 50 nights)

Number of possible weekday rentals: 23,600
(200 sites x 118 nights)

Number of units expected to rent (from the Goal Setting form)  _____

Price that can be charged per unit (use competitor averages and industry trends to figure a reasonable site rental fee for next season)                                                           _____

This approach assures that you'll have an adequate budget for effective marketing. Obviously, an effective marketing program doesn't guarantee you'll make a profit. But it is certain that a profit will never be made if you don't have effective marketing.

# Step 3: Setting the Budget

You now know how many dollars you need to spend to run your campground. In the budgeting step, you'll be determining exactly how many marketing dollars you need to spend per campsite.

Of all the steps in the marketing process, setting the budget is by far the most difficult one on which to be objective. That's why our marketing plan recommends the unit-pricing method — a relatively simple way for you to build your marketing costs into each campsite rental.

Fixed Costs: You need first to figure your campground's break-even point. Start with your fixed cost per campsite. (To figure your fixed cost per campsite, divide your total fixed costs by the number of campsites you have available). Very simply, it costs you a set amount every year to be able to offer that one campsite, whether you rent it or not. Assume, for example, the total fixed cost of running your camp ground is $200,000 a year, including loan payments, general office expenses, maintenance, insurance, taxes, salaries, etc. You have 200 campsites available, so the fixed cost of offering each campsite is $1000 a year ($200,000 divided by 200).

Variable Costs: Next, add in all the variable costs involved in renting that site. Variable costs include the additional expenses you incur (extra utilities, etc.) when that site is actually in use. Use the next year's projections you recorded on the Forecasting form. Multiply the average number of nights you will rent an individual campsite by the extra cost per night. For example, say you have determined that every time you rent a campsite, it costs you an additional $2 per night for utilities and other services. If you have forecasted that you'll be able to rent that campsite out for 100 nights during the next season, your total variable cost for that campsite will be $200 ($2 per night x 100 nights).

Discretionary Costs: Finally, add the money you will need to market each campsite. You can use percentages of your other costs to figure the discretionary cost of marketing. Industry averages or your previous year's marketing costs will help you decide on a reasonable percentage of money to dedicate to marketing. Plan to spend five to ten percent of the total of all the other costs on marketing.

The simple formula for total cost of each campsite will be

Fixed Cost + Variable Cost + Marketing Cost= Total Cost of each site (Discretionary Cost)

Total Cost (of each site) + Profit = Price charged to each customer

Note that we haven't yet figured your profit into this. That's because profit really has nothing to do with figuring out what you need to spend for marketing. In fact, profit is a result of marketing.

Using the previous example, your total cost per campsite would now be

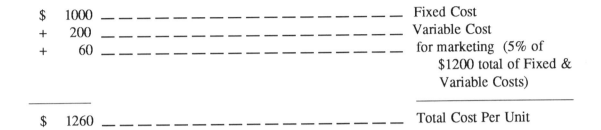

|   |   |   |
|---|---|---|
| $ | 1000 | Fixed Cost |
| + | 200 | Variable Cost |
| + | 60 | for marketing (5% of $1200 total of Fixed & Variable Costs) |
| $ | 1260 | Total Cost Per Unit |

Using the total cost, you can now figure out how many days you must rent that campsite to cover all your costs, not including profit. If you charge $14 per day, you need to rent the campsite for 90 days to break even. For every day you rent that campsite after the first 90, you will be realizing a profit of $11.80 (the $14 charge minus the $2.20 variable cost you have figured per rental day).

You now know how many campsite rentals you must make during the year to cover all your costs. You also know how many dollars you have available to market your campground (the marketing cost per site times the number of sites). In the example above, your marketing budget is $5,400 ($60 per site x 90 sites).

This may be the right amount for marketing, or it may be too much or too little. From Chapter One, you already have an idea of what it will cost to advertise in camping magazines. Media advertising, though, is only one of your marketing costs. Also included in your marketing budget will be the costs of printing and mailing brochures and other literature, attending trade shows, providing promotional items, etc.

To determine whether or not your marketing budget is adequate and realistic, use your figures to work backwards. First, look at competitors' rental prices for campsites similar to yours. Take the average of that range and multiply times the number of nights you project you can rent each site.

For example, assume competitors are renting similar sites for $12 to $16 per night, for an average price of $14 — in this case, the same price you planned to charge. You've projected that you can rent your campsites for 100 nights next season. Multiplying the total rental nights (100) by the average price ($14), you can figure a total income of $1400 per campsite. Now subtract your actual costs ($1260 for fixed and variable costs) from that figure to determine what's available for marketing that campsite:

$1400    -    $1260    =    $140
(income)    (costs)    (Available for marketing and profit)

In your original calculations, you figured 5% for marketing, for a total of $60 per campsite. You've now discovered that you can afford more for marketing of each campsite, and still realize a profit. You have an additional $80 per campsite available.

## Using the Budgeting Form

These steps have been simplified on the Budgeting Form. Go through each step on the form, applying your own figures and percentages to determine your break-even point and your marketing budget. You may need to adapt the numbers to meet your special campground situation; use the principles explained in the examples to make these decisions.

Now compare the figure you arrived at in (p) with the prices charged by your competitors. Keep in mind that your competitors may not have taken a very scientific approach to setting their own prices—they may well have made a guess based on what the park down the road charges. These comparisons will, however, give you an idea of the price the market will bear for site rentals. If yours is lower than the average, is it possible for you to raise it to increase your profit and dedicate more funding to marketing? If it's considerably higher than the average, you may want to reconsider the amount you will spend for marketing.

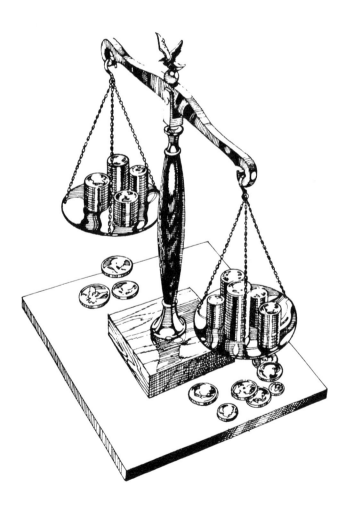

## BUDGETING FORM: DETERMINING THE BREAK-EVEN POINT

(a) $ _____ Total fixed cost (from page 26)

(b) $ _____ Total variable cost (from page 26)

(c) $ _____ Total operating costs (add the two figures)

(d) Number of sites you have available to rent _____

Divide (c) Total operating costs by (d) number of sites to determine (e) cost per unit

$ _____ + $ _____ = $ _____
(total cost per              (marketing cost              (break-even
unit—e)                      per unit—x)                  cost—y)

$ _____(s) x $ _____(p) = $ _____(z)
(number of sites            (price you expect            (available for mar-
expected to rent)           to charge                    keting
                            per site)                    and profit)

# Step 4: Timing and Planning

Now that you know what you have available for marketing, you're ready to decide on when, where and how you will spend it. To time your expenditures, start by filling out your season calendar on pages 34–

## Using the Planning Form

Decide which customer groups are most important in your marketing plan and divide up your marketing budget among the groups you have defined. If you want RV customers to make up 75% of your sales next year, then be sure you allocate 75% of your marketing budget to promotions to this group.

Now consider all the advertising and promotional activities you would like to direct to each customer group during the year. Estimate the cost of each of these activities and fill out the dollar amounts on the form. You can use the forms you filled out in Chapter One to determine costs for media advertising. Ask for quotes from suppliers for the cost of literature and other promotional activities. Trade show costs can be estimated from the information provided by the sponsoring organization and from the totals you spent in previous years.

In some cases, your defined customer groups can "share" allocations of marketing dollars. You may be able to use the same marketing activity to promote your campground to RV customers and to tent campers, for instance, so divide out the costs and note the portion that applies to each customer type.

35. If your campground is open from April 1 to November 1, fill in those months. Calculate the number of weekdays and weekend days in each month and note them here.

Now go back to your Season Calendar and note when you will be carrying out the marketing activities you have decided on. If there's a trade show or community event that you'll be participating in, indicate it under the appropriate month. If you plan on mailing out brochures before or during the season, note this on the form. Think about when you will have opportunities for sending out news releases and which months would be best for advertising in the camping magazines.

If this is the first year you are developing a marketing plan, your decisions about which marketing activities you will participate in may be based on your "feel" for what's needed and on what you can afford. In future years, though, this plan will be self-correcting. You'll have a built-in method for evaluating what you've done and for making future decisions. You'll find that you can easily increase your rentals and income without significantly increasing your marketing budget.

## PLANNING FORM

| | | | |
|---|---|---|---|
| MARKETING BUDGET per CUSTOMER TYPE | $ _____ | $_____ | $_____ | $_____ TOTAL MKTG BUDGET |

COSTS

| | | | | |
|---|---|---|---|---|
| AD PRODUCTION | \_\_\_\_\_ | \_\_\_\_\_ | \_\_\_\_\_ | \_\_\_\_\_ |
| ADVERTISING MEDIA | | | | |
|   MAGAZINES | \_\_\_\_\_ | \_\_\_\_\_ | \_\_\_\_\_ | \_\_\_\_\_ |
|   YELLOW PAGES | \_\_\_\_\_ | \_\_\_\_\_ | \_\_\_\_\_ | \_\_\_\_\_ |
|   DIRECTORIES | \_\_\_\_\_ | \_\_\_\_\_ | \_\_\_\_\_ | \_\_\_\_\_ |
| TRADE SHOWS | | | | |
|   SPACE RENTAL, DISPLAY, TRANSPORTATION, MISC. | \_\_\_\_\_ | \_\_\_\_\_ | \_\_\_\_\_ | \_\_\_\_\_ |
| DIRECT MAIL | \_\_\_\_\_ | \_\_\_\_\_ | \_\_\_\_\_ | \_\_\_\_\_ |
| LITERATURE | | | | |
|   BROCHURE | \_\_\_\_\_ | \_\_\_\_\_ | \_\_\_\_\_ | \_\_\_\_\_ |
|   FORM LETTERS | \_\_\_\_\_ | \_\_\_\_\_ | \_\_\_\_\_ | \_\_\_\_\_ |
|   MAPS | \_\_\_\_\_ | \_\_\_\_\_ | \_\_\_\_\_ | \_\_\_\_\_ |
|   PRICE LIST | \_\_\_\_\_ | \_\_\_\_\_ | \_\_\_\_\_ | \_\_\_\_\_ |
|   OTHER | \_\_\_\_\_ | \_\_\_\_\_ | \_\_\_\_\_ | \_\_\_\_\_ |
| NEWS RELEASES | \_\_\_\_\_ | \_\_\_\_\_ | \_\_\_\_\_ | \_\_\_\_\_ |

| Season Calendar | | | | | |
|---|---|---|---|---|---|
| Item | Jan | Feb | Mar | Apr | May |
| Product Production | | | | | |
| Trade Show | | | | | |
| Literature | | | | | |
| Advertising Media | | | | | |
| News Release | | | | | |
| Spec Sheet | | | | | |
| Other | | | | | |

| JUN | JUL | AUG | SEP | OCT | NOV | DEC |
|-----|-----|-----|-----|-----|-----|-----|
|     |     |     |     |     |     |     |
|     |     |     |     |     |     |     |
|     |     |     |     |     |     |     |
|     |     |     |     |     |     |     |
|     |     |     |     |     |     |     |
|     |     |     |     |     |     |     |
|     |     |     |     |     |     |     |

# 3 GETTING THE WORD OUT: PLANNING YOUR ADVERTISING CAMPAIGN

Many people think of "advertising" as the appearance of an advertisement in a magazine. But advertising includes a number of other ways to communicate with campers and promote your campground. Your advertising can take the form of not only space in publications, but also brochure mailings, newsletters, news releases, road signs, participation in trade shows and all the other ways you send persuasive messages to your potential customers.

This chapter will show you how to evaluate and choose among these various forms of advertising and use a planned campaign to unify all your efforts.

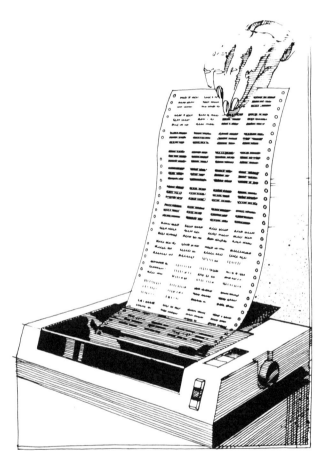

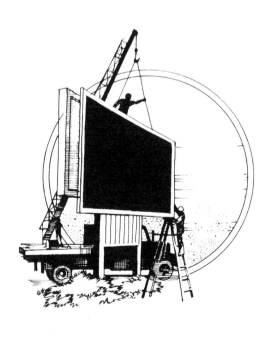

# STEP 1: CHOOSING ADVERTISING ACTIVITIES

You've already done much of the research and planning that will be the basis for making decisions about how to advertise your campground. As with all other elements of your marketing plan, the key to planning effective advertising goes back to the "who"— your definition of the customer from Chapter One. Think about what you already know:

• You have a good idea of who your best potential customer is.
• You have already determined where your customer is.
• You know how much you can spend to reach him or her (from your budgeting decisions in Chapter Two).
• You know what the customer wants, what your competitors are offering him or her and how they are saying it.

With that information in mind, you want first to make decisions about which forms of advertising will be most effective in getting your sales message to your customer. There are many types of media you might use. The ones you choose will depend on your customer definition, the marketing objectives you have already set and the work you want your advertising to do in meeting those objectives.

Here's an overview of the main types of advertising media available to you and the benefits each can deliver in your marketing plan.

## Magazine Advertising

From your Media Analysis in Chapter One, you're already familiar with the camping magazines that are available to you and the specific ones your potential customers are reading. These magazines and newsletters offer you a way to communicate with a group of people who share a common interest, whether it be camping or traveling in general or one specific type of camper, as in recreational vehicles. The more closely an individual magazine's readership matches your definition of your customer, the more cost-effective it will be as an advertising tool.

Magazine advertising can help you accomplish two main types of communications goals in your marketing plan. First, because it's a printed medium, a magazine offers you the opportunity to give detailed information about the benefits your campground offers. Readers of camping magazines and other specialized publications actually seek out the advertising — one of the reasons they read the magazine is for information on the campgrounds and recreational opportunities that are available to them. A magazine ad is also a timely form of communication — your message can be tailored to the time of year you're running your ad. If you're promoting a special event or seasonal rate, you can run your ad in the monthly issue that corresponds most closely to the time you want your customer to have that information.

A second major benefit of magazine advertising is that it helps you create an image or reputation for your campground. This is accomplished through continuity — scheduling ads so your audience receives messages from you at regular intervals. In each ad you run, the details you provide on your campground's location, facilities and services help your potential customers make short-term decisions about where to stay on their upcoming camping trips.

Each individual ad also contributes to the customer's awareness and overall impression of your campground. Over time, the types of messages you send, the information you include and the "look" of your ads will build an image for your campground and keep your name in the customer's mind.

# Direct Mail

One of the primary rules for selling anything is to communicate often and well with your best prospects. Despite the relatively high cost of postage, using direct mail makes sense when you consider the benefits. In addition to getting information to the specific people who are most likely to become paying customers, direct mail can help you

- Tell campers about recent improvements or new services.
- Distribute updated brochures, price lists and other information.
- Promote special events to specialized groups of customers.
- Encourage repeat visits from past customers.
- Develop new groups of potential customers.
- Conduct your own customer survey.

The biggest advantage of direct mail is that it's a personalized form of communication. An envelope, newsletter or brochure with the customer's name on it demands attention. You and you alone are talking to the customers, so you can tailor your message to their special situations.

Direct mail also offers you a great deal of flexibility in choosing what the customer receives and when he or she will get it. You get to decide the following aspects.

## The Type of Mailer

Your mailing can be a single "self-mailer" piece — an address label on a brochure or flyer, for instance — or a package of information in an envelope. The package could include a personalized letter, a brochure, a coupon, a reply card, a promotional gift or any combination of items that can be mailed. Your mailing might take the form of a campground newsletter that is mailed at regular intervals. Whatever type of mailing you choose, you can design it in the size, color and format that best fits your own needs.

## Timing

Direct mail is the most timely of all advertising media. You can send out information to coincide with the beginning of your campground season, the introduction of a new facility or service, a special event, a limited-time offer or your participation in a trade show. And you can mail at any time — you don't have to meet someone else's schedule or production deadlines.

## Class of Mail

You also have some options for controlling your postage costs. If you're sending out newsletters or packages of information to a big group of customers, use a third-class bulk rate to save money. You can apply for your own third-class permit from the post office or, if you're using a mailing service, often you can mail under its permit. For personalized letters or a mailing to a small group, use first class mail to add both speed and "prestige" to your message.

## Trade Shows

The term "trade shows" applies to opportunities you have for face-to-face communication with your potential customers away from the campground. These include everything from camping industry shows and meetings to local camping "expos" or shopping mall exhibits. Your participation in these activities provides a number of benefits in your advertising and marketing program. Your participation in a trade show offers you the opportunity to

- Engage in personalized, two-way communication with prospective customers.
- Conduct customer surveys and gauge attitudes about your campground.
- "Showcase" your campground — your exhibit can include large photos and detailed information about your features that wouldn't be possible to communicate in an advertisement or direct mail piece.
- Increase overall awareness of your campground and create a positive public relations image.
- Get information out on a specific promotion or special event at your campground.
- Generate a mailing list of potential customers.
- Conduct "market intelligence" — by visiting other campground's exhibits, you can learn more about your competitors and get new marketing ideas for your own campground.
- Educate and train new staff members.

The cost of participating in trade shows can be relatively low, especially for local and regional shows that don't involve large travel expenses for you and your staff. To take full advantage of the benefits of these activities, you should plan on promoting your participation before the show and doing follow-up afterwards. Pre-show publicity can include promoting your participation in your regular magazine ads or direct mail materials, mailing personal invitations to key customers and sending out news releases. After the show, you can use a follow-up mailing to thank exhibit visitors and offer a personal invitation or special inducement to visit your campground.

## Other Publications and Listings

Your listings or display ads in the Woodall Camping Directory, your local yellow pages, community directories and other publications can be effective forms of advertising. When evaluating these publications, consider how well their readership matches your definition of your customer and how many potential customers they can deliver for your dollar. You may also be able to take advantage of "free" customer referrals through your local chamber of commerce, tourism office and other groups. Do some research to find out what listings and services are available in your area and how you can participate.

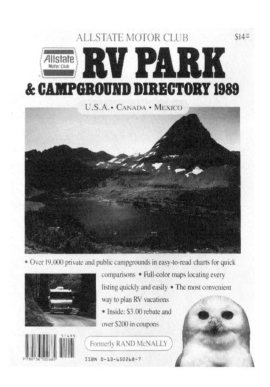

## News Releases

News releases are individual stories or short announcements about anything new related to your campground. Because they are news stories, there's no charge for their appearance in the publications that print them for you. You can take advantage of this free publicity by sending out news releases — as many of them as you can generate and as often as you can — to local newspapers, group newsletters, national camping magazines and other industry publications.

What has "news value" on your campground? News can include information about almost anything that is new and of interest to the readers of the publication to which you're sending the news release. You can use news releases to publicize

- The introduction of new facilities or services at your campground.
- Your participation in a trade show or community event.
- The availability of speakers for community groups.
- New staff members or promotions.
- Contest winners.

## Personal Selling

Personal selling efforts are also a form of advertising because, like other media, they are a way of conveying information about your campground to potential customers. Your "sales calls" might involve sending a campground staff member to speak at local group meetings or to contact representatives of local, regional or national camping groups. Just like other forms of advertising, direct selling — and sales follow-up activities — should be evaluated in terms of how effective they will be in getting your message to your defined customers. If the cost of direct selling justifies the potential results, it should be included in your advertising budget.

## Outdoor

Outdoor advertising includes paid space on billboards as well as your own road signs. This form of advertising can provide several benefits for your campground, including the following:

1. They increase your name recognition by providing a regular reminder of where you are and what you offer.
2. They show travelers how to get to your campground.
3. They reach your defined customers with your message at a key time — on the highway, when they may be making a decision about where to camp. You can display your message on established billboards by renting the space from the outdoor advertising company that owns the structures. If you're considering designing and erecting your own signs, be sure to check out your state and local ordinances first. They may limit or even prohibit new signs in some locations.

## Television and Radio

Compared to other forms of advertising, the broadcast media will probably offer limited benefits in your advertising campaign. If you think of your advertising costs in terms of the number of defined customers you reach for each dollar you spend, radio and television usually won't "deliver" as many potential customers as the more specialized media will. Because they have such wide, varied audiences, you'll be paying to talk to people who aren't your defined customers.

In some special circumstances, though, you may want to consider the value of local broadcast media, especially radio. If your campground is participating in a local recreational event or offering a special promotion to area groups, radio commercials can be a very cost-effective way of getting the word out to the community-at-large.

## "Word-of-Mouth Advertising"

A word — and a warning — about "word-of-mouth" advertising: "It's the best advertising I've got" is frequently heard from small business owners who believe good word-of-mouth advertising can do all the work necessary to market their products. There's no question that a network of personal referrals is a valuable form of communication. The problem comes when it's the only advertising you've got.

That's because positive word-of-mouth advertising doesn't reach as many potential customers as most business owners believe. In fact, its only significant impact comes when it's negative. If campers like your campground and have an enjoyable experience during their stay with you, they're likely to share that news only if someone asks them about it directly. But if they have a bad experience, the details about it will be more interesting to their friends and acquaintances — your unhappy campers will probably volunteer the details to anyone who will listen.

# STEP 2: TIMING THE CAMPAIGN

Before you prepare your advertising materials, you should think of all your activities in terms of an advertising campaign that ties all your activities together. A campaign is simply a road map for your advertising to follow — a continuous program that appears over a period of time and re-emphasizes a consistent theme.

Use the Advertising Campaign form shown on pages 44–45. Go back to the Season Calendar and Planning forms you prepared when figuring your marketing budget in Chapter Two. On those forms, you outlined your camping season and the timing of your major advertising and marketing expenditures. Use this information as a guide for planning and timing each of the advertising activities included in your campaign. Fill in the months of your camping and/or advertising season. If you're planning mailings or other advertising during the off-season, note the approximate time on the form. For each category, note the specific advertising activity and relevant dates (General Ad; Memorial Day Promotion Ad; Pre-season Newsletter; Camping Expo, May 3-5; etc.). For one-time activities (such as brochure production and listings in the yellow pages or other publications), note when your deadlines are and when the customer will receive the message.

You'll realize a number of benefits from planning your campaign in this way. Among them,

- You'll save money. By knowing your advertising needs in advance, you can better anticipate the costs and avoid waste. It also allows you to buy media space, production materials and supplies in quantity.

- You can achieve consistency, which is vital to the success of your advertising. A planned campaign helps you maintain a high level of customer awareness and unify your messages with a common theme.

- You'll be able to make better media decisions by seeing your advertising as a continuous effort over a period of time.

## ADVERTISING CAMPAIGN FORM

|  | JAN | FEB | MAR | APR | MAY |
|---|---|---|---|---|---|
| MAGAZINE ADS |  |  |  |  |  |
| TRADE SHOWS |  |  |  |  |  |
| NEWS RELEASES |  |  |  |  |  |
| YELLOW PAGES |  |  |  |  |  |
| OTHER PUBLICATIONS |  |  |  |  |  |
| BROCHURES |  |  |  |  |  |
| DIRECT MAIL |  |  |  |  |  |
| OUTDOOR |  |  |  |  |  |
| DISTRIBUTION OF SPECIAL PROMOTIONAL ITEMS |  |  |  |  |  |
| RADIO |  |  |  |  |  |
| ROAD SIGNS |  |  |  |  |  |
| OTHER: |  |  |  |  |  |
| OTHER: |  |  |  |  |  |
| OTHER: |  |  |  |  |  |

| JUN | JUL | AUG | SEP | OCT | NOV | DEC |
|-----|-----|-----|-----|-----|-----|-----|
|     |     |     |     |     |     |     |
|     |     |     |     |     |     |     |
|     |     |     |     |     |     |     |
|     |     |     |     |     |     |     |
|     |     |     |     |     |     |     |
|     |     |     |     |     |     |     |
|     |     |     |     |     |     |     |
|     |     |     |     |     |     |     |
|     |     |     |     |     |     |     |
|     |     |     |     |     |     |     |
|     |     |     |     |     |     |     |
|     |     |     |     |     |     |     |
|     |     |     |     |     |     |     |

# STEP 3: SCHEDULING MEDIA

Now that you have selected the types of advertising you want to do and planned your campaign for the year, you're ready to make final decisions about when and how your advertising actually will reach the customer. This includes selecting specific publications and monthly issues for your magazine advertising, deciding the size and frequency of ad insertions and other decisions involved in placing paid advertising with the media.

In Chapter One, you evaluated the various publications and recorded information about their audiences, costs and publication schedules. You can use that information now to make specific decisions about which publications and issues to advertise in, the size of your ads, how often they will appear and other scheduling details. Some of the factors you will want to consider (and the media terms used) include the following:

Vehicle — a specific publication or source of advertising space or time. Trade journals are a type of media; *Camping Madhouse* is a media vehicle.

Cost-per-thousand— the cost of reaching 1000 of your defined customers with a single ad in that publication, based on the media vehicle's advertising rate and readership.

Continuity — a method of scheduling advertising so that audiences have an opportunity to see ads at regular intervals. Continuity can be achieved with a series of ads in the same vehicle or with the use of various media that reach the same potential customers. This consistency is important in building a reputation and maintaining customer awareness of your campground.

Volume (or "Reach") — the number of people who will see one message.

Frequency — the average number of times each individual will be exposed to your advertising messages during the year.

Some of your media selections will be made on a fairly subjective level. You're the expert on your campground, so don't be afraid to trust your instincts about which media and which vehicles are "right" for reaching your customers. When deciding among your alternatives, though, there are some time-tested objective guidelines you can use to come up with the best selections. Some major considerations for print advertising follow.

## Cost-per-thousand

For almost all of your media decisions, the major determining factors will be the definition of your customers and the most cost-efficient way of reaching them. How can you get your message to the greatest number of your defined customers for the least amount of money? Camping magazines and other publications have already figured this out for you, and the numbers seldom lie. Their cost-per-thousand figures — both for total readership and for various categories of readers — tell you what it costs in advertising dollars to talk to your customers. *Camping Madhouse* may be your favorite magazine, but if the numbers tell you that your defined customers like a different one better, then that's where your advertising dollars should go.

## Frequency vs. Volume

Should you try to reach the greatest number of potential customers once (volume) or send many messages to a smaller number of customers (frequency)? When frequency and volume are compared, frequency will win almost every time. One big media splash at the beginning of your campaign may give you a high volume of readers, but your message is soon forgotten. Instead, aim for continuity by emphasizing frequency in your advertising. Regular contact with customers throughout the year will deliver a consistent, lasting message that enhances the effectiveness of your advertising campaign.

## Ad Size

The size of the space you buy in a publication affects both your advertising costs and the impact of your message. An ad that's too small may not attract enough attention, and an ad that's too big will be a waste of money. In deciding on ad size, think about what you have to say and show and the "look" you want for your ad. In general, you should try to buy slightly more space than you need for your message — an ad with some open space (white space) will look less cluttered and attract more reader attention. You can also use your competitors' ads in the publication as a guideline. If you want your campground's advertising to have a similar impact, aim for the same size; if you want to draw significantly more attention to your ads, then buy a bigger size.

## Using the Media Planning Form

The Media Planning form is included on pages 48–49 to help you break your campaign schedule down by specific supplier. If you're advertising in more than one publication or using several different types of media, you can use this form as a scheduling calendar. Once you've filled in the individual media purchases you have planned, the form will also give you a specific breakdown of your advertising campaign activities and a closer look at the exact timing and frequency of your messages to your potential customers.

# Media Planning Form

| | Jan | Feb | Mar | Apr | May |
|---|---|---|---|---|---|
| Publication | | | | | |
| Publication | | | | | |
| Publication | | | | | |
| | | | | | |
| Direct Mail | | | | | |
| Sales Calls | | | | | |
| Follow-up | | | | | |
| News Releases | | | | | |

| Jun | Jul | Aug | Sep | Oct | Nov | Dec |
|---|---|---|---|---|---|---|
|  |  |  |  |  |  |  |
|  |  |  |  |  |  |  |
|  |  |  |  |  |  |  |
|  |  |  |  |  |  |  |
|  |  |  |  |  |  |  |
|  |  |  |  |  |  |  |
|  |  |  |  |  |  |  |
|  |  |  |  |  |  |  |

# 4 PUTTING IT IN PRINT: PREPARING YOUR PRINT ADS AND NEWS RELEASES

## Writing and Preparing Print Ads

Whatever medium you're using, an effective advertising message elicits four responses or actions from the person to whom it's directed:

Attention — it captures customers' attention and makes them want to read the rest of the ad.

Interest — the message holds their interest by telling them something relevant and meaningful about the product.

Desire — the ad creates a want or need for the product in customers' minds.

Action — the ad "moves" customers to buy the product.

Your first concern in preparing an advertisement, then, is whose attention, interest, desire and action are you interested in? That brings you back to your definition of the customer from Chapter One.

Buying decisions are usually made one person at a time, so think of your advertising audience as one "typical" individual. By knowing who that person is and what motivates him or her, you can talk the right language and tell the person what he or she needs to know.

In this chapter, you'll learn more about how to write and design your advertising messages so they reach the customer with the greatest impact possible.

# STEP 1: DECIDING WHAT YOUR AD CAN—AND CANNOT—DO

You've already made decisions about who to talk to and when, where and what to advertise. Before actually preparing an individual advertisement, it's a good idea to think specifically about the "why" behind the ad, too. What is your specific purpose in running this ad? What do you want it to accomplish in your advertising campaign and in your overall marketing plan?

There are a number of ways an ad can help persuade potential customers to become your paying customers. Among other things, an ad can

- Increase awareness of your campground's existence
- Remind customers of the availability of your facilities
- Create a desire for a special feature or facility you're offering
- Convince customers that your campground offers an advantage over competitors' campgrounds
- Give customers information on how to find your campground and become your customers
- Give information about a special offer or promotion
- Create a long-term image or reputation for your campground

Notice that all of these "abilities" of advertising concern something that happens in the customer's mind. By themselves, your advertising messages don't really increase your sales or profits, at least not directly. Instead, they help persuade the potential customer that your campground offers something desirable, and that's what leads him or her to make a buying decision. In other words, an advertisement should be designed to communicate, not to "sell." If you think about your ads in this way, you'll have a clearer idea of what information to include and how to say it.

If you have a feature or facility that customers would enjoy, your advertising can tell them about it and create a desire for it in their minds. One thing your advertising can't do, however, is convince customers to buy something that they inherently don't want. The best ad in the world can't persuade campers that a major disadvantage of your campground is actually desirable. Similarly, advertising can't "educate the market" about the value of something that doesn't fit in with customers' current lifestyles or camping equipment. If you have a campground without RV hookups, for example, no amount of advertising will convince RV owners to come to your campground and rent tents.

So be glad that you have competitors, because their advertising helps promote the use of all campgrounds. And when something brand new comes along, it will be the industry as a whole that educates the market and makes it desirable.

## STEP 2: WRITING THE PRINT AD

Before preparing a magazine ad or a display ad for a camping directory, be sure you have up-to-date information on the publication's requirements — closing date for ad submissions, publication date, ad size specifications, mechanical requirements for production, etc.  You probably collected most of this information in your Media Analysis in Chapter One.  It can be found in the SRDS (Standard Rate & Data Service) publications in your library.  A source easier to use is the publication's media kit, which you can request directly.  Or you can take advantage of media sales representatives who will call on you personally and assist with ad submissions.

Once you have all the technical requirements, you're ready to write your copy and design the ad. This chapter will give you tips on developing the four main elements of a print ad:

1. Headline — the large type, usually at the top of the ad, which the reader sees first.

2. Copy block — the smaller type, below the headline, which gives more detailed information about your campground.

3. Logo — the name, address and phone number of your campground, along with any art or symbol you use to "identify" your campground.

4. Visual and layout — any art, photos or design elements used in the ad and the placement of these in the ad space.

Before you write any copy, go back to Step 4 of Chapter One, where you determined the one key feature, benefit or advantage that you could use to promote your campground to your defined customer. Emphasizing this "Key Benefit" is the secret to writing an effective advertising message — it will communicate one main selling idea to your potential customers and set your campground apart from your competitors.

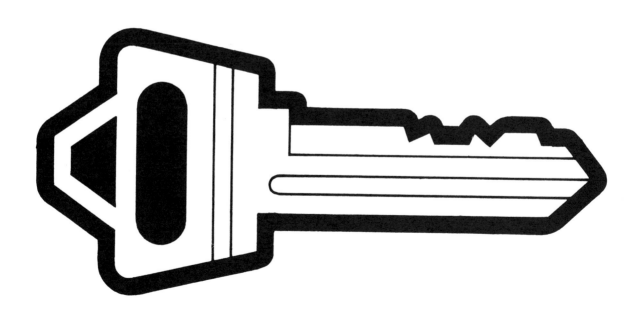

### Writing the Headline

Put the Key Benefit in the headline. Many campground ads, especially those in directories, rely on just the name of the campground as the headline. For a stronger message, try to incorporate your Key Benefit into the headline. This will send an immediate sales message to your customer and differentiate your ad from others.

Appeal to your specific audience. Remember that the purpose of your ad is to offer a benefit to your defined customers, so don't be afraid to write a headline that's of interest only to them. A headline that identifies a specific type of customer may "lose" other readers, but it will improve readership by the people you're most interested in talking to. Some examples:

- "Closest RV Park to Atlanta" — if your Key Benefit is proximity to a big city and your defined customers own RVs.

- "Arkansas' Largest Wilderness Tent Campground" — if you're trying to attract more tent campers.

- "Spectacular Fall Foliage — at a special weekend rate for seniors" — if the purpose of your ad is to promote an autumn discount for senior citizens.

Keep it short and simple. Your headline doesn't have to say everything — only enough to make your potential customers interested in your campground. Use as few words as possible to communicate a benefit, attract attention and make your customers want to read the rest of your message.

Make it stand out. Depending on how long your headline is, use type that's large enough to set it apart from the rest of the body copy. Try not to let the headline run into the other ad elements — surround it with some extra space to draw the reader's eye to it.

# Arkansas' Largest Wilderness Tent Campground

# Modern camping comforts
# in an *old world* atmosphere

## Closest RV Park to Atlanta

## Spectacular Fall Foliage

### Special Weekend Rates for Seniors

## Writing the Body Copy

Relate the copy to the headline. If you've mentioned your Key Benefit in your headline, you should explain it further in your body copy. Use the copy to re-emphasize the benefit or provide more details about how to take advantage of it. This unifies your message and gives the customer a clearer idea about what sets you apart from your competitors.

Use bullets for a list of features. In addition to your Key Benefit, the body copy can also highlight other advantages of your campground. If you want to include more than two or three other features, consider using a "bulleted" list instead of writing them out in a paragraph. This will help break up the copy and give potential customers quick, easy-to-read information about your facilities. Speak to the individual customer. When writing the body copy, think of your potential customer as one person and write directly to him or her. Personalize the copy — emphasize "you" rather than "campers," "we" rather than "the campground." Aim for a conversational tone by using contractions, "action" verbs and present or future tense (instead of past tense).

Make every word count. Keep your copy as short as possible and select the words carefully to be sure they're meaningful to the potential customer. Try to avoid cliches, overworked sales lingo and words and expressions being used by other campgrounds. "The finest in camping," "You're always welcome" or "Get away from it all" don't say anything of substance to your potential customers — but "Enjoy our heated swimming pool," "Secluded campsites on the lakeshore" or "Featuring 300 acres of hiking trails" tell them something of interest. Some other tips for writing professional copy:

- Use "exciting," descriptive adjectives — try to come up with alternatives for vague words like "nice," "interesting," "great."

- Don't exaggerate, brag or use too many superlatives ("the most," "the largest," etc.). If your copy contains too many of these, your reader will tend not to believe any of them.

- Use your campground name in the copy. Even though your campground is identified at the bottom of the ad, using your name in the body copy will reinforce the reader's association of your name with the benefits you're offering.

- Make your copy clear and easy to read. Avoid overuse of italics, quotation marks, capitalization, exclamation points, leaders ( . . . ), sentence fragments and other extra punctuation. These copy "gimmicks" often draw attention away from the information in your copy and interfere with the reader's understanding of your ideas.

- Use a strong closing. At the end of your copy, before your campground name and address, include a "call to action" that asks the customer to visit your campground or call for reservations.

modern facilities

quaint serenity

secluded lakeside setting

spacious tent sites

full-service RV hook ups

# STEP 3: ADDING YOUR CAMPGROUND LOGO

Make your name stand out. The logo, which includes your campground name, location and telephone number, is usually placed at the bottom of the ad. Make the name of your campground the most prominent feature of this part of the ad. If you're requesting that customers call for reservations, the phone number also should stand out from the other information. You can do this by setting the name or number in larger type, by using color or by placing extra space around the type.

Use an identifier. To establish your campground "identity" and provide continuity, your logo should have the same look in all your advertising. Continued use of a distinctive typeface is an easy way to do this. Or you may want to use a symbol or other artwork to give your logo a unique look. Some campgrounds also use a slogan or short line of copy along with the logo on all their ads. Ideally, this copy should be short and descriptive and provide a clear association with your Key Benefit.

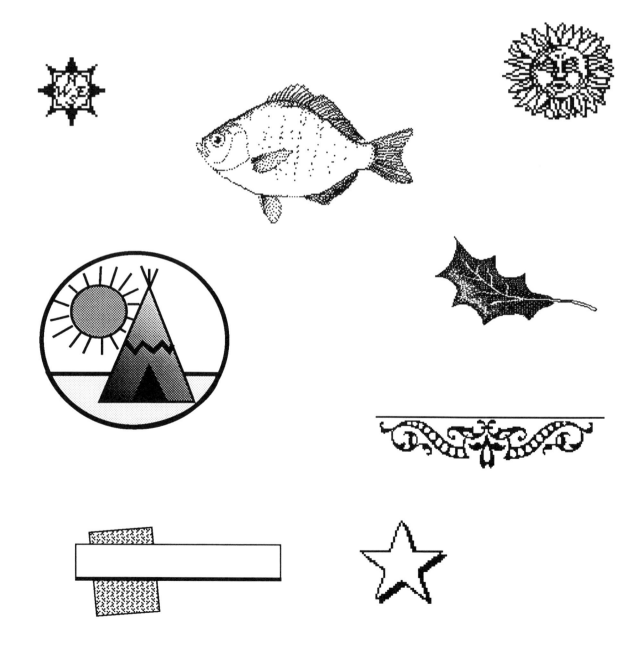

# STEP 4: DESIGNING THE LAYOUT

Follow the publication's requirements. Before you begin laying out your ad design, be sure the size, art and other elements you're using will conform to the publication's mechanical requirements.

Make the visual relevant. If you're using a visual — a photograph, illustration or other artwork — be sure it relates to the headline and body copy.

Use white space. White space is simply blank space in the ad layout. It's usually used around the outside edges of the ad and around the headline, visual and logo. Using ample white space opens up your layout and draws the reader's eye to the other elements of your ad. It's also one of the best ways to make your ad stand out from others around it. This is a special problem in campground directories, where your ad may get lost in the "clutter" of several other campground ads on the page.

"Open up" the copy. If you have a relatively long copy block, you can increase readership by breaking it up visually. The bulleted list is one way to do this. You can also open up the copy with subheads, short paragraphs, space between paragraphs and wide margins.

Revise ad elements to fit your space, or vice-versa. After writing your copy and selecting visual elements, sketch out the full layout, estimating the size of the copy and other elements. Look at the overall visual impact of your rough sketch. If your layout lacks white space and appears crammed with information, you should either omit something or buy a larger space. If you can't afford to buy more space, start deleting copy or visual elements. A cluttered, heavy look will discourage potential customers from reading any part of your ad. Your first purpose is to attract the reader's attention, so it's better to leave out some information than to cram too much into a small space.

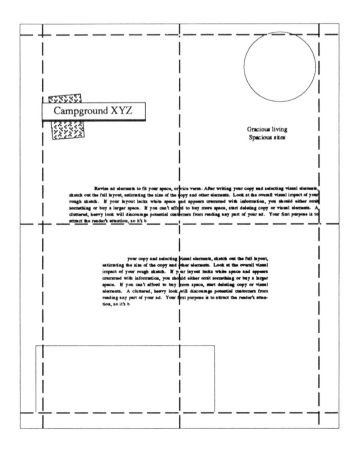

# STEP 5: EVALUATING YOUR AD

## The VIPS Test — Elements Your Ad Should Have

When putting all the elements together, evaluate the overall effect in terms of the "VIPS" formula. Your finished ad should have

Visibility — The ad should stand out from the rest and stop the potential buyer. This can be accomplished with the use of a photo, an attention-getting headline, an attractive layout, anything that draws attention to your ad.

Identity —The ad should clearly identify the name of your campground. The reader should be able to make a quick, clear association between the Key Benefit and your campground.

Promise — The ad should emphasize and explain a benefit or "reward" you're offering to the potential customer.

Simplicity — You should use the fewest number of words and design elements possible to communicate your Key Benefit.

If your ad is weak in any of the above, go back and make changes. Reword the headline or copy to make them clearer, eliminate unnecessary words, "open up" the look by removing design elements or copy blocks, choose a larger size type for your logo.

If possible, get the reactions of some of your defined customers before you send the ad to the magazine. Ask your campers if the ad would catch their attention in a camping magazine, if you've highlighted the features that are important to them, if there's anything in the ad they don't understand. Their comments may help you fine-tune your copy and layout so the ad will get the response you want.

Art work around
border to add
visual interest

White space
to draw attention

Benefit in
headline

More information
on the benefit

Another feature
that's important
to the customer

Bullets to set
off a list

Identifying
symbol
and type
for logo

Identifying
slogan used
in all
advertising

Box to highlight
phone number

# *INDIAN LAKE CAMPGROUNDS*

**Modern camping comforts**
in an *old world* atmosphere.

You'll enjoy the quaint serenity of the Amish countryside along with the most modern facilities at Indian Lake Campgrounds, the newest campground in Illinois' historic Amish settlement. Our secluded lakeside setting offers over 100 spacious tent sites and full-service RV hook-ups. Indian Lake campers also enjoy

- Canoe trips, hayrides and buggy tours of Illinois Amish Country
- Weekend Amish festivals and fairs in the villages
- Nearby Rockome Gardens Park and Amish Family Restaurant
- 26 antique and craft shops within 10 miles
- Campground Country Store
- Stocked fishing lake — no license required

*INDIAN LAKE CAMPGROUNDS*
In the heart of Illinois Amish Country

Three miles west of Highway 30 on
Country 1040 W
Arthur, Illinois

For a free Amish Country map and camping guide, call:
**800-555-2367**

## Writing News Releases

News releases are news stories written by you and submitted to the press — usually to camping publications, newsletters and local newspapers. To take advantage of this free publicity, think about what is "news" on your campground. It can be a special event, a new facility, your participation in a trade show or anything else that is timely and of interest to the readers of the publication. (A description of news releases and more ideas for stories are included in Chapter Three.)

### Step 1: Writing the Lead Paragraph

To organize your information, think in terms of the six questions that journalists always answer when writing news stories: Who? What? When? Where? Why? How?

The first paragraph of your news story is the "lead" and should include as many of these "Five Ws and an H" as are relevant. Make the lead paragraph short — no more than one or two sentences.

### Step 2: Writing the Full Release

To write the rest of the story, organize the information so the most important facts appear early. The last paragraph should contain the least important information because editors cut stories from the bottom to fit the space they have available.

Your finished release should be the following:

Concise — Make the release as short as possible to increase your chances of having it published. Use short, descriptive words and be as direct as possible. Try to make paragraphs no longer than four or five typewritten lines.

Objective — Your story should sound like news, so report only facts. Avoid using words or expressions that sound like advertising copy —in a news story, you won't get away with saying that your campground is offering a "fantastic" promotion or that it offers the "utmost in modern camping conveniences."

Precise — Make the facts as specific as possible. Don't say "many" if you can say 100; don't say "this month" if you mean "during May."

Timely — Think about when your story actually will be published, and word the information so it is relevant at the time your reader will see it. Allow plenty of lead time, especially if you're submitting your story to a monthly publication. Your local newspaper will usually publish your release within a week, but a monthly publication will need to have your story at least 6-8 weeks before it will be published.

### Step 3: Submitting the Release

When submitting your release to the publication, use the guidelines below to prepare the final copy. A sample release in the correct format is included in this chapter.

* Type the release, double spaced, on one side of the page only.
* In the upper left-hand corner, type your campground name, your name, address and phone number.
* In the upper right-hand area of the page, indicate the topic of the release ("ABC Campgrounds Receives Award") and the time the news should be printed ("For Immediate Release" or "For Release After May 1").
* Separate the heading from the story with a line.
* Indicate the end of the story by typing or drawing a # mark below the last line.
* If your story runs more than one page, type or write "more" at the bottom of the first page, centered a few lines below the last line on the page. On the second page, type a short heading with the topic and page number ("ABC Campgrounds - p. 2").

**SAMPLE NEWS RELEASE**

Indian Lake Campgrounds
Joe Brown
R. R. 3
Arthur IL                                        For Immediate Release
(217) 555-2367                                   Amish Quilt Show

— — — — — — — — — — — — — — — — — — — — — — — — — — — — — — — — — —

More than 100 handmade quilts will be on display at the Indian Lake Campgrounds' Amish Quilt Show and Craft Fair on Labor Day weekend, September 1 and 2, 1990. This annual event, which is free to campers and the public, will be held at the campground's Lake Park Pavilion near Arthur, Illinois.

In addition to the quilt show, the weekend will feature demonstrations of quilt making, weaving, pottery making and chair caning by local Amish artisans. Twenty local shops will be offering antiques, crafts and baked goods for sale. Buggy ride tours of Amish country will also be available. Beginning at 7:00 p.m. on Saturday, visitors can participate in special demonstrations of Amish apple butter making. The campground will host a hot dog roast and hayride beginning at dark on Saturday.

Indian Lake Campgrounds is located three miles west of Highway 30 on County 1040W near Arthur, Illinois. Overnight camping is available for over 100 recreational vehicles, pull-thrus and tent campers. Indian Lake campers will receive discounts on craft shop merchandise at the show.

#

# 5 MAKING YOUR MARKETING EFFORTS PAY OFF: HANDLING INQUIRIES AND FOLLOW-UP

At this point, all the work you've done on your campground's marketing plan is in motion and your efforts are paying off. You're sending the right message to the right customers and you're generating demand for your campground's services. But this is no time to sit back and just wait for the campers to come in. To complete the marketing circle, you need to turn that customer interest into real business for your campground. If you don't have an organized, effective system for following up on customer inquiries, then all your other efforts have been wasted.

It sounds simple. A potential customer finds out about your campground from your ad or another source and calls or writes you for details. You answer questions on the phone or send a brochure. If your services, prices and location fit in with what the camper is looking for, he or she becomes your paying customer.

However, a good follow-up system involves more than just supplying requested information. To provide the greatest marketing benefits, your system should be able to keep track of information about not only potential campers, but also your current customers.

Organizing information about both types of customers will give you the answers to a number of important questions and actually will help you accomplish many of your marketing tasks. An effective follow-up system will help you do the following:

- Locate your customers. Defining your customer is a continuous process — you need good information on your current customers to help you refine your definition for the future. The inquiries you receive will tell you exactly who your real customers are and whether you have defined them correctly.

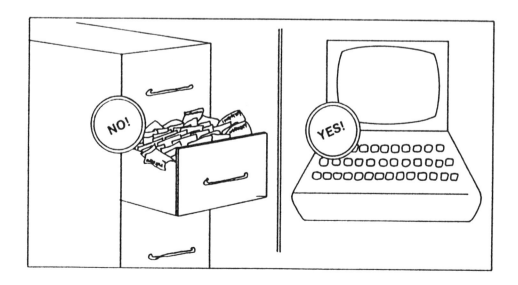

63

- Plan your budget. The numbers and types of inquiries you receive will help you make accurate sales forecasts.
- Select advertising media. You'll know which camping magazines are reaching the greatest number of your defined customers.
- Improve your advertising messages. Inquiries generated by your ads in camping magazines will tell you which of your ads are creating the most interest. The types of questions you get from potential campers will tell you what your advertising copy should highlight.
- Handle your direct mail campaigns. Names, addresses and other customer information can be easily organized to improve the effectiveness of your direct mailings. You can generate a list of customers by type and automatically print out mailing labels.

How can you take advantage of all these benefits? You must have a controlled system for obtaining information from your customers and for retaining and organizing that information for future use. Many campgrounds already have the beginnings of a system in place — when campers register, they fill out forms that list name and address, type of camping equipment and other relevant information. Unfortunately, these forms are often filed away in a drawer and pile up into such a mountain of paper that it becomes impossible to organize the information for any marketing purpose.

The "average" U.S. campground has over 9400 customers a year. Even if that's in families of three or four, that's over 3000 customer transactions — too many for you to keep track of in a file drawer. The solution — and it's an easier one to implement than you might think — is a computerized system that stores this information and automatically organizes it for your purposes.

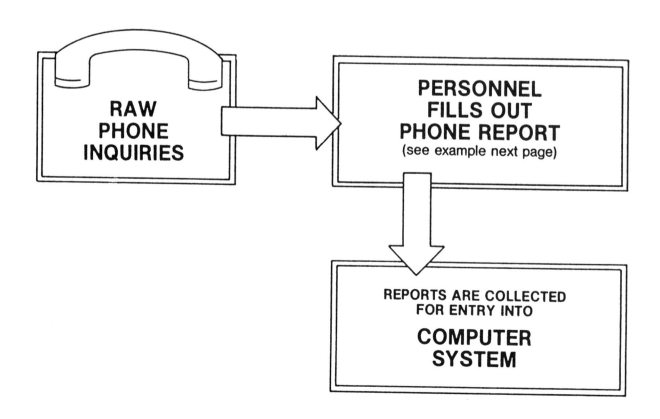

# CREATING YOUR FOLLOW-UP SYSTEM

## Setting It Up

Obviously, the first step in your system is to get the hardware and software you need to handle all the work. You may already have a personal computer in your campground office. If you don't, it's an investment you need to make and one that will pay for itself by saving time for you and your staff, improving the efficiency of your marketing efforts and, ultimately, increasing your business. The heart of your system is the software program that handles the information, so if you don't have a computer already, shop for the software before you buy the hardware. You can choose from a wide variety of available software packages that are pre-programmed to handle all the jobs your campground might require. Check the ads in camping journals and magazines and send for various companies' demonstration packages. Try out these demo programs on a friend's computer or take them to the computer store where you're planning on buying your hardware. Try out the demos there and select the package you want to buy. Then let the computer salespeople help you determine what type of computer you need to run that program. Most of the software packages you try out will probably include far more than you need to handle your marketing follow-up. In addition to keeping track of your customers, they typically include capabilities for handling your accounting, inventory, payroll, reservations and other business tasks. It really doesn't matter whether you want to use the programs for these functions or not — even if you use only the customer base and mailing list programs, the software will be worth your investment.

*A Typical Software Package*

One of the campground management programs now on the market is Camping II, which is distributed by the National Campground Owners Association (NCOA). It includes a comprehensive set of programs for handling reservations, calculating visitor fees, recording transactions, printing financial reports, organizing tax information and accomplishing other campground management tasks. Its main benefit in your marketing plan is its customer data program. The program organizes almost any type of information you want to record on individual campers, including

Name and address

Names and addresses of extra persons on the site

Type of camper and site

Vehicle identification

Length of stay

Past visits

Payment history

Trouble encountered during a stay

Future reservations

How they learned about your campground

Other customer categories (ages, group affiliations, etc.)

Once this data is stored, the program offers you a wide range of ways to use it — in both day-to-day operations and overall marketing efforts. When a return customer checks in, for instance, you instantly can display data about the individual's previous visits, including "trouble reports" that will help you anticipate needs for the current stay. Its customer summaries show you which types of customers are using your campground, how long they're staying, how often they return, what problems they're encountering, how they found out about your campground and almost anything else you request.

The Camping II software includes built-in help screens like the one on the opposite page to help you take full advantage of the program's capabilities.

---

**MAILING LIST HELP SCREEN**

---

Help Screen


### *** MAILING LABELS REPORT ***


This report provides mailing labels for all customers with whom you have done business from the entered date to present.


If a state is specified then only customers from that state will be reported. Leaving the state field blank will report on all customers in the database. Up to five marketing codes may be specified to select customers with those codes in the 'Referred by' field of the customer data. You may also exclude customers with trouble reports.


Select the sort order to be either last name or zip code. The report may be directed to your printer (PRN) or a disk file.


The disk file name is mailing.rpt.


Press the <F10> key to create the report. If you are using the printer, make sure that it is on and is on-line.


You may alter the format of this report by editing the form MAILING.


End of Help Text      Press Spacebar to Continue

Camping II includes screens like the one on the opposite page for you to record a wide range of information on every customer who makes a reservation at your campground. For mailing labels for your direct mail campaigns, the program will select names from the customer database to match the categories you specify.

Like other software programs on the market, Camping II includes a manual and a tutorial that takes you through all the steps involved in making the program work. Phone support is also available. For more information on Camping II or demonstration diskettes, contact

NCOA
11706 Bowman Green
Reston, VA 22090
(703) 471-0143.

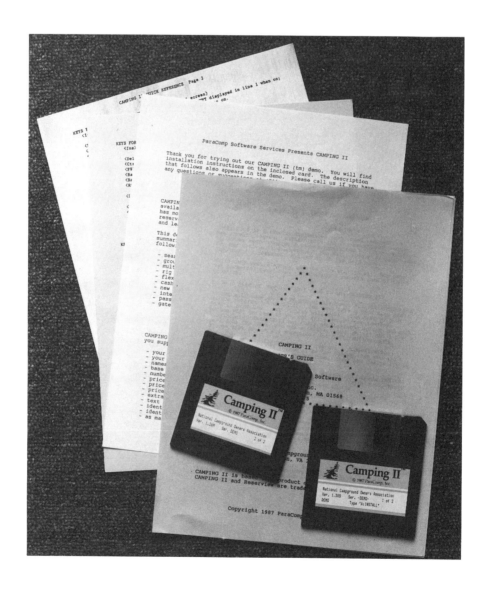

---

### CUSTOMER INFORMATION SCREEN

---

Customer Info

First Name        John                Last Name      Smith




Street address        141 Hill St
City  Champaign        State  IL          Zip      61820
Foreign country
(Area) phone #        (217)  123-4567
Referred by      Peter Mason
Notes        Needs mooring for sailboat
Car make/model        Nissan. . . .          Regis WF  1895.
. . . . . .

Type   vehicle  identification.  Type  <F10>  to  save,
<F2>  for  new,  <F8>  when  done.

<Esc>  back  up   <Ctrl><End>  clear  to  end
  <Arrows>move      <Return>  go  to  next

F1-HELP    F2-NEW    F5-PREV    F6-NEXT    F7-DELETE
F8-DONE       F9-CLR       F10-SAVE

## Making the System Work

You'll be using your system to store and organize information on your current customers and your potential customers — those who show an interest in your campground by calling or writing for information.

*Current Customers*

For your current customers, some of the types of information you will want to record are discussed in the section on software packages above. The best way to start this process is to have your customers fill out a form that includes the categories of information you want to record. You can use a pre-printed form similar to the one shown here, or you can design your own. At the end of the day (or the week, or whenever you have the time), key this information into your software program. It takes only a few seconds per customer, and the information will be stored for a wide variety of future uses.

| | |
|---|---|
| **PLEASE PRINT** | **SITE NO.** |
| NAME | |
| ADDRESS — PHONE | |
| CITY — STATE — ZIP | DATE IN |
| CAR | DATE OUT |
| LIC. NO. — STATE — MAKE | YEAR |

HOW DID YOU HEAR OF US?
☐ C.G. Directory ☐ Hwy. - Road Signs ☐ Camping Show
☐ Friends ☐ Phone Directory ☐

☐ FIRST VISIT
☐ RETURN VISIT

| | |
|---|---|
| **NUMBER IN FAMILY** Adult Child Guest Pets | Camping Fee $ |
| **NOTICE TO GUEST** This property is privately owned. We reserve the right to refuse service to anyone and will not be responsible for accidents or injury to our guests or for loss of money or valuables of any kind. **THE MANAGEMENT** | Electric & Water $ |
| | Sewer $ |
| | Additional Persons $ |
| | Total Daily Charges $ |
| I AGREE TO READ AND COMPLY WITH ALL CAMPGROUND RULES AND REGULATIONS AS POSTED IN THE OFFICE AND/OR ON THE GROUNDS. | No. Nights X $ $ |
| | $ |
| N° 5000 | SUB-TOTAL $ |
| | Tax $ |
| | TOTAL CHARGES $ |
| X | Less Advanced Deposit $ |
| **CAMPER'S SIGNATURE** | **BALANCE DUE** $ |

MYRTLE Jenkins Business Forms, Mascoutah, IL 62258    Rev. 9/87

*Potential Customers*

You'll be receiving inquiries about your campground from many sources, including

- Ads in camping magazines
- Listings in campground directories
- Press releases in camping magazines and local newspapers
- Displays at trade shows or camping fairs
- Referrals from current customers

When an individual inquiry comes in — whether it's a phone call, letter or reply card — record all the relevant information: who that person is, what he or she asked about, what prompted the inquiry, etc. A sample form for recording information from telephone requests is shown here. Use small tablet-sized sheets, and keep them near all your phones so your staff can use them easily. The customer information on the forms can be entered into the computer later. You can develop a similar form for mail inquiries, or you can key the information into the computer program when the inquiry arrives. Keep track of how you followed up on the inquiry, too. The software will keep track of this and can show you what worked and what didn't — how many callers who received brochures actually made reservations, for example.

## TELEPHONE FORM

NAME: _____    DATE _____

ADDRESS: _____

CITY/STATE/ZIP: _____

TYPE OF CAMPING EQUIPMENT: _____

WHERE CALLER LEARNED OF CAMPGROUND:

    DIRECTORY LISTING: _____

    MAGAZINE AD: _____

    MAILING: _____

    CAMPING SHOW: _____

    REFERRAL (FROM): _____

    OTHER: _____

SUBJECT OF CALL (SPECIFIC INFORMATION REQUESTED): _____

LITERATURE SENT: _____

## Using the Information for Direct Mail

One of the many benefits of a computerized system is its ability to plan and carry out direct mailings to the types of customers you specify. Direct mail is frequently used to respond to inquiries from potential customers. It's valuable also for developing repeat business — you can use mailings to invite individuals back to your campground, inform them of new campground features or services, offer them special promotions or discounts.

With the computer, the most difficult part of a direct mail campaign is handled automatically. Maybe you've decided you want to offer a special discount or referral incentive or other promotion to just one type of customer — RV campers who have sent you inquiries, families who stayed more than one night, senior citizens, etc. The program will save you money by generating a list that identifies just the people you specify and will even print the mailing labels. All you have to do is determine what you want to send and affix the labels and postage.

The flexibility of direct mail in general and your campground software program in particular allows you to send almost any type of literature you like to any type of customer. The direct mail package can include a personalized letter, price list, campground brochure, brochures from local attractions, discount coupons, referral forms — whatever you think will appeal to the customers you have chosen.

Pre-season mailings to past or potential customers can be especially effective. These mailings will reach your customers when they're making plans for the camping season. They can be used to remind customers of your campground, update your prices and features or offer a discount or promotional item.

A sample pre-season letter is shown on page 74. It would be mailed to all campers who visited the campground during the previous year and would be accompanied by a new brochure, price list and discount coupon.

Like many other software packages, Camping II will automatically print a letter to confirm reservations. With the letter, you can send out a brochure, price list or other promotional literature.

## EVALUATING YOUR SUCCESS

The marketing circle is now complete. You've made a marketing plan and put it into action, and now you have a system for handling all the new business you've created. What's left for you to do? Marketing is a continuous process, so you never really can sit back and just let it happen. As you carry out your marketing activities, you'll see which parts of your plan are working well and which need improvements. At the end of your camping season or marketing year, you'll want to evaluate your plan and its results and make decisions for the coming year.

The best way to refine your plan is to go back to Chapter One and use this book to go through each element of your plan again. Start with blank forms and fill them out for the next year, making any needed changes in your customer definition, competitor and campground evaluations, budget, advertising campaign, media plan, sales forecasts — everything that affects the way you market your campground to your customers. The answers you come up with will be the basis for building even more success into your marketing plan for the coming year.

---

**SAMPLE PRE-SEASON LETTER**

---

*INDIAN LAKE CAMPGROUNDS*
In the heart of Illinois Amish Country
Three miles west of Highway 30 on County 1040W
Arthur, IL

March 1, 1990

Mr. Phil Fillman
111 W. Hill
Champaign IL   61820

Dear Mr. Fillman:

As a recreational vehicle owner, no doubt you're looking forward to the upcoming camping season. We hope you enjoyed your stay with us last year and that you'll join us again in 1990.

We've added a number of new facilities since your last stay at Indian Lake, including ten new full-service recreational vehicle pads. We're also planning a number of special events this year that you'll want to put on your camping calendar. They include

**RV Expo**
**May 2 & 3, 1990**
Over twenty dealers from throughout the Midwest will be displaying their 1990-91 models in the Indian Lake Park. Special discounts will be available to overnight campers.

**Fourth of July Party**
**July 3 & 4, 1990**
Indian Lake Campgrounds is famous for its annual fireworks show, and this year's will be bigger and better than ever.

**Amish Quilt Show & Craft Fair**
**Labor Day Weekend, September 1 & 2, 1990**
Crafts and antique buffs won't want to miss this weekend. In addition to the display of handmade Amish quilts, the fair will feature an antique flea market and demonstrations by local artisans. Buggy rides, an apple butter bee, square dancing and old-fashioned hayrides complete the fun.

As a special thank you for your past patronage, we've enclosed a discount coupon you can use during your first 1990 stay at Indian Lake. It entitles you to 15% off any site rental for two nights or more.

Indian Lake Campgrounds will be open beginning April 1, 1990. A 1990 brochure and price list is enclosed — please call me at 1-800-555-2367 if you need more information or would like to make a reservation. We hope you'll join us soon.

Sincerely,


Joe Brown

---

### SAMPLE CONFIRMATION LETTER

---

*INDIAN LAKE CAMPGROUNDS*
In the heart of Illinois Amish Country
Three miles west of Highway 30 on County 1040W
Arthur, IL

April 17, 1990

Ms. Karen Walker
111 W. Hill
Champaign IL 61820

Dear Ms. Walker:

Thank you for your reservation. We look forward to your arrival on 05/15/90. Your site is reserved for 4 day(s) with checkout scheduled for 05/19/90. We have received $ 0.00 toward your bill. The balance of $ 68.00 will be due at check-in.

If you have any questions or need anything further, please give us a call at 1-800-555-2367.

Sincerely,


Joe Brown

# FORMS

The forms which have been discussed throughout this guide are duplicated in the following section. The forms in this section are blank on the reverse so that readers may remove the forms without also removing pertinent information.

| | | Potential Customers | Week-Day | Week-end | Percentage for Year | Distance They Traveled to Get to Your Facility |
|---|---|---|---|---|---|---|
| 1. | Tents | | | | | |
| 2. | Pop Up/ Pull Up Campers | | | | | |
| 3. | Trailers | | | | | |
| 4. | Pickup Truck Mtd | | | | | |
| 5. | Trailers | | | | | |
| 6. | 5th Wheel | | | | | |
| 7. | RVs | | | | | |
| 8. | Motorcycles | | | | | |
| 9. | Groups | | | | | |
| 10. | Other | | | | | |
| 11. | Other | | | | | |
| 12. | Other | | | | | |

**Customer/Market Definition Form**

# MEDIA ANALYSIS FORM

PUBLICATION _____  _____  _____

EDITORIAL PROFILE _____  _____  _____

_____  _____  _____

_____  _____  _____

_____  _____  _____

EDITORS _____  _____  _____

_____  _____  _____

REP YOUR AREA _____  _____  _____

COST B&W PAGE _____  _____  _____

CPM* _____  _____  _____

FORMAT: PAGE SIZE _____  _____  _____

PUBLICATION FREQUENCY _____  _____  _____

DEADLINE _____  _____  _____

CIRCULATION _____  _____  _____

CONTROLLED _____  _____  _____

PAID _____  _____  _____

• • • • • • • • • • • • • • • • • • • • • • • • • • • • • • • • • • •

PRIMARY CIRCULATION _____  _____  _____

_____  _____  _____

_____  _____  _____

_____  _____  _____

_____  _____  _____

_____  _____  _____

TOTAL _____  _____  _____

*CPM FORMULA: $\frac{\text{COST} \times 1,000}{\text{CIRCULATION}}$ = COST PER THOUSAND (CPM)

| COMPETITOR ANALYSIS FORM | | | | |
|---|---|---|---|---|
| | DATE RECEIVED | | MATERIALS RECEIVED | |
| CAMPGROUND | P | B | PERSONAL INQUIRY | BINGO |
| | | | | |
| | | | | |
| | | | | |
| | | | | |
| | | | | |

PRODUCT EVALUATION FORM

TYPE OF CAMPER: _____

[ ] Current Customer          [ ] Potential Customer

QUESTIONS:

1. Do you understand the main features and benefits being offered by the ABC campground?

    [ ] Yes    [ ] No

2. Which features of the campground are most beneficial to you?

_____
_____
_____
_____

3. What campground features do you consider to be disadvantages?

_____
_____

4. Based on what you know about the ABC Campground, would you consider staying at ABC?

    [ ] Yes    [ ] No    *(If YES, please answer Question 5)*

5. If you would be interested in camping at ABC, when would you be most likely to use the campground?

    [ ] Summer vacation
    [ ] Other: _____
    [ ] Weekend getaway      [ ] Weekdays

    How often would you use the campground?

          [ ] Once a year     [ ] Twice a year     [ ] Three times a year or more

    How long would your stay be?

          [ ] One night only     [ ] 2 to 3 nights     [ ] 4 nights or more

## ANALYSIS FORM

DESCRIBE CUSTOMERS:

| | CAMPER TYPE | HOW MANY | DISTANCE TRAVELED |
|---|---|---|---|
| 1. | | | |
| 2. | | | |
| 3. | | | |
| 4. | | | |

DESCRIBE COMPETITOR:

| | CAMPER TYPE | NUMBER UNITS | PRICE RANGE |
|---|---|---|---|
| 1. | | | |
| 2. | | | |
| 3. | | | |
| 4. | | | |

COMMON DENOMINATORS: _____

_____

_____

_____

_____

## GOAL SETTING FORM

TYPE OF DEFINED CUSTOMER: _____

CAMPGROUND LOCATION: _____

_____

SHORT-TERM GOALS:

1. _____

2. _____

3. _____

4. _____

LONG-TERM GOALS:

1. _____

2. _____

3. _____

4. _____

## FORECASTING FORM

### LAST YEAR

Number of units rented     _____
(One day's rental of one site is a unit.
Total units rented is the number of
campsites multiplied by the total number
of days each was rented).

Number of weekend days campsites were
  rented     _____
(Number of campsites multiplied by
the number of weekend days they were
filled)

Number of weekdays campsites were
  rented     _____
(Number of campsites multiplied by
the number of weekdays they were
filled)

### NEXT YEAR

Total possible rentals     _____
(Add up the total number of calendar
days your campground is open during
the year by the number of campsites)

Number of possible weekend day
  rentals     _____
(Count the number of weekend days
during the campground season and
multiply by the number of campsites
you have available)

Number of possible weekday
  rentals     _____
(Count the number of weekdays
during the campground season and
multiply by the number of campsites
you have available)

Number of units expected to rent     _____
(From the Goal Setting form)

Price that can be charged per unit     _____
(Use competitor averages and industry
trends to figure a reasonable site rental
fee for next season)

---

**BUDGETING FORM: DETERMINING THE BREAK-EVEN POINT**

---

(a) $ _____ Total fixed cost (from page 26)

(b) $ _____ Total variable cost (from page 26)

(c) $ _____ Total operating costs (add the two figures)

(d) Number of sites you have available to rent _____

Divide Total (c) operating costs by (d) number of sites to determine (e) cost per unit

$ _____ + $ _____ = $ _____
   (total cost per       (marketing cost       (break-even
       unit—e)           per unit—x)         cost—y)

$ _____(s) x $ _____ (p) = $ _____ (z)
  (number of sites       (price you expect     (available for mar-
  expected to rent)        to charge             keting
                   per site)          and profit)

## PLANNING FORM

MARKETING BUDGET
PER CUSTOMER TYPE          $ _____    $_____    $_____    $_____

                                                                        TOTAL
                                                                        MKTG
                                                                        BUDGET

COSTS

AD PRODUCTION              _____    _____    _____    _____

ADVERTISING MEDIA

   MAGAZINES              _____    _____    _____    _____

   YELLOW PAGES           _____    _____    _____    _____

   DIRECTORIES            _____    _____    _____    _____

TRADE SHOWS

   SPACE RENTAL, DISPLAY,   _____    _____    _____    _____
   TRANSPORTATION, MISC.

DIRECT MAIL               _____    _____    _____    _____

LITERATURE

   BROCHURE               _____    _____    _____    _____

   FORM LETTERS           _____    _____    _____    _____

   MAPS                   _____    _____    _____    _____

   PRICE LIST             _____    _____    _____    _____

   OTHER                  _____    _____    _____    _____

NEWS RELEASES             _____    _____    _____    _____

## Season Calendar

| Item | Jan | Feb | Mar | Apr | May |
|------|-----|-----|-----|-----|-----|
| Product Production | | | | | |
| Trade Show | | | | | |
| Literature | | | | | |
| Advertising Media | | | | | |
| News Release | | | | | |
| Spec Sheet | | | | | |
| Other | | | | | |

99

| Jun | Jul | Aug | Sep | Oct | Nov | Dec |
|-----|-----|-----|-----|-----|-----|-----|
|     |     |     |     |     |     |     |
|     |     |     |     |     |     |     |
|     |     |     |     |     |     |     |
|     |     |     |     |     |     |     |
|     |     |     |     |     |     |     |
|     |     |     |     |     |     |     |
|     |     |     |     |     |     |     |

## Advertising Campaign Form

| | JAN | FEB | MAR | APR | MAY |
|---|---|---|---|---|---|
| MAGAZINE ADS | | | | | |
| TRADE SHOWS | | | | | |
| NEWS RELEASES | | | | | |
| YELLOW PAGES | | | | | |
| OTHER PUBLICATIONS | | | | | |
| BROCHURES | | | | | |
| DIRECT MAIL | | | | | |
| OUTDOOR | | | | | |
| DISTRIBUTION OF SPECIAL PROMOTIONAL ITEMS | | | | | |
| RADIO | | | | | |
| ROAD SIGNS | | | | | |
| OTHER: _____ | | | | | |
| OTHER: _____ | | | | | |
| OTHER: _____ | | | | | |

| JUN | JUL | AUG | SEP | OCT | NOV | DEC |
|-----|-----|-----|-----|-----|-----|-----|
|     |     |     |     |     |     |     |
|     |     |     |     |     |     |     |
|     |     |     |     |     |     |     |
|     |     |     |     |     |     |     |
|     |     |     |     |     |     |     |
|     |     |     |     |     |     |     |
|     |     |     |     |     |     |     |
|     |     |     |     |     |     |     |
|     |     |     |     |     |     |     |
|     |     |     |     |     |     |     |
|     |     |     |     |     |     |     |
|     |     |     |     |     |     |     |
|     |     |     |     |     |     |     |

## Media Planning Form

| | Jan | Feb | Mar | Apr | May |
|---|---|---|---|---|---|
| Publication | | | | | |
| Publication | | | | | |
| Publication | | | | | |
| | | | | | |
| Direct Mail | | | | | |
| Sales Calls | | | | | |
| Follow-up | | | | | |
| News Releases | | | | | |

| JUN | JUL | AUG | SEP | OCT | NOV | DEC |
|-----|-----|-----|-----|-----|-----|-----|
|     |     |     |     |     |     |     |
|     |     |     |     |     |     |     |
|     |     |     |     |     |     |     |
|     |     |     |     |     |     |     |
|     |     |     |     |     |     |     |
|     |     |     |     |     |     |     |
|     |     |     |     |     |     |     |
|     |     |     |     |     |     |     |

---

## Telephone Form

Name: _____  Date _____

Address: _____

City/State/Zip: _____

Type of camping equipment: _____

Where caller learned of campground:

    Directory listing: _____

    Magazine ad: _____

    Mailing: _____

    Camping show: _____

    Referral (From): _____

    Other: _____

Subject of call (specific information requested): _____

Literature sent: _____